FEARLESS COACHING

RESILIENCE AND RESULTS FROM THE CLASSROOM TO THE BOARDROOM

DOUGLAS REEVES

WITH
LISA ALMEIDA
TONY FLACH
KATE ANDERSON FOLEY
AMANDA GOMEZ
JO PETERS
BILL STERNBERG

Copyright © 2023 Creative Leadership Press

All rights reserved. No part of this book may be used or reproduced by any means, graphic, electronic, or mechanical, including photocopying, recording, taping or by any information storage retrieval system without the written permission of the author except in the case of brief quotations embodied in critical articles and reviews.

This book is a work of nonfiction. Unless otherwise noted, the author and the publisher make no explicit guarantees as to the accuracy of the information contained in this book, and in some cases, names of people and places have been altered to protect their privacy.

Archway Publishing books may be ordered through booksellers or by contacting:

Archway Publishing
1663 Liberty Drive
Bloomington, IN 47403
www.archwaypublishing.com
844-669-3957

Because of the dynamic nature of the Internet, any web addresses or links contained in this book may have changed since publication and may no longer be valid. The views expressed in this work are solely those of the author and do not necessarily reflect the views of the publisher, and the publisher hereby disclaims any responsibility for them.

ISBN: 978-1-6657-3519-3 (sc)
ISBN: 978-1-6657-3518-6 (hc)
ISBN: 978-1-6657-3520-9 (e)

Library of Congress Control Number: 2022923125

Print information available on the last page.

Archway Publishing rev. date: 05/10/2023

For the teachers and educational leaders around the world
who still believe in our students and our schools.

CONTENTS

Acknowledgments		xiii
Introduction		xv

PART I. THE EVIDENCE: WHY FEARLESS COACHING WORKS

Chapter 1.	What Makes Fearless Coaching Different?	5
	What Does "Coaching" Mean, Anyway?	6
	Why Fearless Coaching Is Different	7
	Defining The Real Client	13
	How To Identify And Avoid Ineffective Models Of Coaching	16
Chapter 2.	The Eleven Biggest Coaching Mistakes: And How To Avoid Them	19
	Coach Fails To Establish Trust With Client	20
	Coach Fails To Define And Stick To Roles Of Coach And Client	21
	Coach Allows Talk As A Substitute For Action	21
	Coach And Client Fail To Define Success In Clear And Measurable Terms	23
	Coach Uses Friendship As A Barrier To Candid Feedback	25
	Coaching Conversations Focus On Uncontrollable Factors	26
	Coach Fails To Understand Personal And Family Crises Of Client	27

	Coach Uses "Smart Talk" To Avoid Discussing Essential Issues	28
	Coach Serves As Expert Consultant, Rather Than Challenging Clients To Build Their Own Expertise	28
	Coach Is Not Prepared For The Session	30
	Coach And Client Fail To Make Their Meetings "Sacred Time"	32
Chapter 3.	The Coach-Client Relationship	34
	Coach Is On The Sidelines, Not In The Game	34
	Coach Notices What Works And What Doesn't	36
	Coach Is Not Invested In Past Practices And Methods	37
	Coach Provides Immediate Clear And Actionable Feedback	38
	Coach Listens To All Of The Players, Not Just The Team Captain	39
	Coach Is Relentlessly Goal-Focused, Linking Actions To Results	41
Chapter 4.	What The Client Should Expect From The Coach	45
	Confidentiality: With Clear Exceptions	46
	Candor: What Works And What Doesn't	47
	Curiosity: Continual Search For The Causes Of Barriers To Success	48
	Confidence: Relentless Advocacy For The Client And The Organization	50
	Clarity: Focusing On The Few Actions That Matter Most	51
Chapter 5.	What The Coach Should Expect From The Client	54
	Availability: Making Coaching Sessions A Priority, Without Interruption Or Multitasking	55
	Openness: Allowing The Coach Access To Data, Teachers, And Students	57
	Interest: Genuine Curiosity About How To Improve Performance	58

Vulnerability: Willingness To Discuss
Organizational And Personal Challenges   60

PART II. PASSION: THE ENERGY THAT DRIVES COACHING SUCCESS

Chapter 6.	Contrasting Visions Of The Future	65
	What Does The World Look Like When Coaching Is Successful?	66
	What Does The World Look Like Without Coaching?	67
Chapter 7.	Sources Of Emotional Energy	71
	Purpose And Meaning	71
	Physical Health	73
	Relationships	74
	Service	76
	Mindfulness	77
	Connection With Children	78
	Self-Efficacy	79
Chapter 8.	Sources Of Emotional Drag	82
	Self-Criticism	83
	Fragmentation	84
	Distance From Children	85
	Learned Helplessness	85
	Loss Of Integrity	87
	Substance Abuse And Addictive Behaviors	88
Chapter 9.	The Power Of Focus	91
	Focus And Student Results	92
	Focus On Personal Satisfaction And Happiness	94
	Focus And Organizational Health	95
	The Power Of The Garden Party And The Not-To-Do List	96
Chapter 10.	Avoiding Initiative Fatigue	99
	The Initiative Inventory	100
	Assessing Implementation	101

Assessing Impact On Results	103
Every Turkey Has A Champion	104

PART III. COACHING TEAMS

Chapter 11. Coaching District Teams And Superintendent's Cabinet	109
The Value Of Great Meetings	111
The High Cost Of Bad Meetings	112
The Science Of Effective Meetings	113
Coaching Teams For Better Meetings	119
Chapter 12. Coaching School Leadership Teams And Teacher Teams	121
The Collaboration Imperative	122
Focus On Learning, Teaching, And Leadership	123
Saving Time With Four-Line Emails	124
Coaching Teacher And Administrator Teams	127

PART IV. RESULTS: REAL-TIME FEEDBACK FOR CONTINUAL ENERGY AND ENTHUSIASM

Chapter 13. Measuring What Matters Most	131
Balancing Causes And Effects	132
The Primacy Of Adult Actions	134
Coaching For Results	135
Chapter 14. Leading Indicators	138
Focused Leadership	141
Effective Classroom Instruction	142
Accurate Feedback For Students	143
Deliberate Practice For Students And Staff	147
Laser-Like Focus On Achievement	147
Collaborative Scoring	148
Comprehensive Nonfiction Writing	150
Explicit Instructional Leadership	151

Chapter 15.	Results Indicators	153
	Attendance	155
	Engagement	157
	Achievement	157
	Growth	159
	Personal Results	159
Chapter 16.	Coaching In A Crisis	162
	Lessons Of The Pandemic	163
	School Violence	165
	Teacher Shortage	166
	Funding Cliffs	166
Chapter 17.	Putting It All Together: From Coaching To The Classroom	168
	Finding The Islands Of Excellence	169
	Meaningful Celebrations	170
	Replication: Expanding The Client's Impact	171
	Do Now: Creating A Sense Of Urgency	172
	Coaching Coaches	173

Afterword: Fearless Coaching and the Greater Good—Four Crossroads for Every Coaching Relationship ... 175
    Persistence Through Adversity ... 176
    Raising The Bar ... 177
    Leveraging Impact Through Others ... 177
    Relentless Focus ... 178

Appendices: Checklists for Coaches and Clients ... 179
    A. Coaching Readiness Checklist: Before the First Call ... 180
    B. First-Meeting Checklist: Building the Relationship ... 182
    C. Coaching Conversations About Root Causes ... 186
    D. Goals Checklist ... 188
    E. Effective Time Management Checklist ... 191

	F.	Leading Collaborative Teams of Teachers and Administrators Checklist	192
	G.	Leading Indicators Checklist	199
	H.	Classroom Observation Checklist	200

About the Author and Contributors   201
References   205

ACKNOWLEDGMENTS

Our first debt is to the educators and leaders who have given us the privilege of working with them as coaches. As with all teachers, we often learn from others far more than we teach. We are especially indebted to our colleagues at Creative Leadership Solutions, an organization that has provided the opportunity to share our research and ideas globally. When the pandemic first hit in March 2020, and it was not clear when or if schools would open and professional learning came to a halt, this amazing team delivered free professional learning to more than 40,000 educators around the world. Their dedication to our profession shines through every day, and I am proud to call them my colleagues and friends. In particular, I wish to acknowledge the excellent support of Fiona Dwyer, our Coordinator of Professional Learning, who helped prepare the manuscript of *Fearless Coaching*, and the exceptional operational leadership of Lauren Mahoney, who continues to skillfully balance the multiple demands on the time of the author and contributors toward writing, speaking, and supporting teachers and leaders in the field.

We owe an intellectual debt to Professor Amy Edmondson of the Harvard Business School for her pioneering work in psychological safety. The evidence she has accumulated in fields as diverse as medical care and airline safety demonstrates that psychological safety is literally a matter of life and death. Additional sources of intellectual inspiration include Teresa Amabile, Jenny Donahoo, Rick DuFour and Becky DuFour, Bob Eaker, Adam Grant, Tom Guskey, John Hattie, Kim Marshall, Cal Newport, and Martin Seligman.

My contributing colleagues deserve special recognition. They include Lisa Almeida, Kate Anderson Foley, Amanda Gomez, Jo

Peters, Tony Flach, and Bill Sternberg—each of whom brought to *Fearless Coaching* a wealth of experience and deep passion for the work. Any remaining oversights are mine alone, and I seek the reader's forgiveness for the inevitable sins of omission and commission.

Douglas Reeves
Boston, Massachusetts
April 2023

INTRODUCTION

This is the essence of Fearless Coaching: When the teacher, team, or leader who is being coached is so psychologically safe that they can learn without fear, they can talk with their coach about challenges and mistakes they have made—and leave each coaching meeting with a profound sense of resilience and confidence. On days when these clients doubt whether they make a positive impact on students and colleagues, the Fearless Coach will provide evidence that their work matters.

This book is divided into the following four parts. Part I reviews the evidence as to why Fearless Coaching works. That is, effective coaching is not solely associated with achieving organizational goals, student achievement, parent engagement, and collaborative learning by faculty members and leaders. Effective coaching is also related to higher levels of emotional and physical well-being by the clients. Fearless Coaches know that the appearance of a school's success can be a pyric victory, because the cost of that success can be burnout and turnover of staff. This challenge is particularly acute in high-poverty schools where one program is piled on top of another, and teachers and administrators strain under the weight of initiative fatigue.

Chapter 1 considers what makes Fearless Coaches different. There are many coaches out there with little in the way of standard practice, leading the Harvard Business Review to refer to coaching as "the Wild West". In these pages, readers will see that Fearless Coaching is a rigorous and systematic approach to helping teachers, leaders, and teams. Chapter 2 reveals the 11 biggest coaching mistakes and how to avoid them. Chapter 3 considers the coach-client relationship. If you are beginning your coaching journey as a client or coach, then

Chapters 4 and 5 are especially important. These chapters specify what the clients can expect from the coach and what the coach can expect from the client.

Part II addresses the subject of passion. This is the energy that drives coaching success. Fearless Coaches are passionate not only about the mission of schools but also about the people in them. Both clients and coaches need deep reservoirs of emotional energy to sustain their work. Chapter 6 concentrates on contrasting visions of the future. The passion required for coaching stems from a powerful vision of the future success of students when teaching and leadership are successful, as well as from an equally vivid vision of the future of students when schools do not succeed. The latter vision lasts not only for a single school year but for decades to come. When students do not leave high school ready for success in the workplace, they face a lifetime of poverty, unemployment, excessive medical-care costs, and involvement in the criminal justice system. Fearless Coaches insist that student success is a public health issue, and we must now take our commitment to student success as seriously as our collective commitment to student health and safety.

Chapter 7 outlines sources of emotional energy, and Chapter 8 details sources of emotional drag. Educators and administrators are frequently so hard on themselves that they fail to recognize the positive impact they have. The Fearless Coach does not flatter the client but is obligated to provide objective feedback on what is working from the classroom to the boardroom.

Chapter 9 considers the power of focus, with striking evidence that there is an inverse relationship between the number of priorities a school and district have and gains in student achievement. Chapter 10 eviscerates the plague of initiative fatigue, a primary source of burnout for teachers and leaders.

Part III is devoted to the special case of coaching teams, from teams of classroom teachers to cabinet officers at school districts, counties, and other jurisdictions. Chapter 11 details the complex challenges of district teams, including the superintendent's cabinet. Those are probably the most expensive meetings in any district, and this chapter details ways in which this time and money can be invested more wisely. Chapter 12 considers the importance of coaching school-level teams, including collaborative teams of teachers and school leadership teams. Since cowriting "The futility of PLC Lite" with the late Rick DuFour, coaching collaborative teams of teachers has provided one of the best returns on investment we have observed. Within just a few months, these teams are proceeding from PLC Lite to effective teams focused on the essentials of Professional Learning Communities: learning, assessment, support, and enrichment. In addition, this team coaching saves time for teachers and administrators by replacing endless forms that divert time away from meaningful collaboration with streamlined four-line emails that correspond to the four questions of a successful Professional Learning Community.

Part IV addresses the issue of results and measuring what matters most. This is far more than test scores but also includes leading indicators—the measurable actions of educators and school leaders and how they support the results that policymakers seek.

Chapter 12 offers a fundamental restructuring of educational accountability from a focus only on effects—typically test scores, attendance, graduate rates, and discipline data—to a focus on causes. This would give schools and districts the liberty to establish more constructive accountability systems that would reveal to policymakers and the public the specific teaching and leadership practices that are most effective in the individual environment, culture, agenda, budget, and labor agreement of each system. Without this essential understanding of the causes of student success, schools are doomed to repeat past practices without insight as to the relationship of these practices to student results. Chapter 14 addresses specific leading indicators that educational systems can monitor, focusing on a few high-leverage practices that have a disproportionate impact on student achievement. Chapter 15 considers the results indicators and how teachers and leaders can draw a straight line from causes to effects.

Chapter 16 discusses how coaching is evolving in the post-pandemic world, recognizing that as this book goes to press in the 2022–2023 school year, it is far from clear that the pandemic is over. Schools will be dealing with the lingering effects of quarantines, absences, learning loss, emotional isolation, and behavioral impacts of the pandemic for many years to come. Fearless Coaches must recognize that when teachers and administrators are facing the crisis of the day, it's hard to reflect on a strategic plan. We therefore insist that the coaching cycle includes not only a long-term vision, but short-term wins that restore the confidence of faculty, leaders, families, and policymakers. The book concludes with Chapter 17, which provides practical ideas on how to transform theory into practice. While the reference section includes abundant citation sources, our experience is that the research that matters most to teachers and building leaders is a systematic analysis of local evidence of impact. The question is not: What works?—but rather: What works right here, right now?

The Afterword addresses why Fearless Coaching matters for the greater good, not only for the students for whom we have direct responsibility but for society at large.

The Appendices include reproducible forms that coaches and clients may wish to use to help them communicate effectively with one another and with their colleagues. There's work to be done, so let's get started.

PART I
THE EVIDENCE: WHY FEARLESS COACHING WORKS

If you want to improve performance for yourself and for your team, then you have come to the right place. Whether the team is a group of teachers, a leadership team, an entire school, a department, or a multi-school educational system, the evidence about the impact of coaching is significant and growing. While the intellectual understanding of leadership and organizational development is interesting, it is the application through coaching that transforms ideas into action. Not only do participants in coaching experience greater psychological well-being, self-regulation, and self-insight as a result of personal coaching, but their team benefits from gains in goal attainment and solution-focused thinking (Grant & Atad, 2021). This book is designed to meet the needs of experienced coaches who want to improve their professional learning and service to clients, for educators and leaders who wish to become coaches, and for system-level leaders who are considering implementing a coaching culture in their schools.

As this book goes to press, there are more than 40,000 books about coaching, so we have an obligation to the reader to explain what makes *Fearless Coaching* different. Coaching as a profession is poorly defined, labeled by the *Harvard Business Review* as "the Wild West"—inconsistent, ambiguous, and without professional standards (Sherman & Freas, 2004). Though there are organizations dedicated to evidence-based approaches to coaching and continual professional learning—such as the Institute of Coaching associated with McLean Hospital and the Harvard Medical School, to which the contributors to this book belong—coaching for educators and leaders remains largely defined by the coaches themselves. That is why, in the following pages, you will find extensive research citations to support our claims about the impact of coaching. Moreover, we distinguish Fearless Coaching because of its unique focus on psychological safety—the essential ingredient to learning, leadership, teaching, and personal growth (Edmondson, 2018; Reeves, 2021b). Too many coaching relationships swing from one extreme of fearfully coddling the client in order to maintain pleasant and unchallenging relationships, to the other extreme—incessantly telling war stories about the coach's personal history and attempting to convince the client that the coach's experience should be replicated. *Fearless Coaching*, by contrast, is a rigorous process of deep listening, objective assessment, and capacity-building in which clients improve teaching and leadership through a greater understanding of the needs of every stakeholder in the systems they serve and a deep recognition of the knowledge and skills that they must acquire and practice in order to meet those needs.

In this book, we will explore the evidence of the impact of coaching from both formal research studies and case studies from our global coaching practice. While the names of the individual clients have been altered, the facts of the cases are unchanged. The results are important, as are coaches and clients. The impact on the individual clients and the schools and educational systems we have helped are consistent. A through-line that connects research from quantitative, qualitative case studies; meta-analyses; and syntheses of meta-analyses is the power of efficacy—the bone-deep belief that the individual has significant influence over results (Reeves, 2020a). When different researchers—using different methods and operating independently—come to the strikingly similar conclusion that the efficacy of teachers, leaders, and students is at the heart of improved student performance, then we have achieved not merely a single research finding, but a preponderance of the evidence as well. While many research findings in education vary widely and results are often ambiguous, the evidence on efficacy is conclusive. Without educators and leaders who have confidence that they influence results, even the best research-based programs will fail. Efficacy is at the heart of educational success, and fearless coaching is at the heart of efficacy.

CHAPTER 1

WHAT MAKES FEARLESS COACHING DIFFERENT?

- ❖ What Does "Coaching" Mean, Anyway?
- ❖ Why Fearless Coaching is Different
- ❖ Defining the Real Client
- ❖ How to Identify and Avoid Ineffective Models of Coaching

IN THIS CHAPTER WE INTRODUCE THE ESSENTIALS OF *FEARLESS Coaching*. We begin with a clear definition of the coaching relationship and then consider what makes this particular type of coaching, with its commitment to psychological safety, different from other forms of coaching that readers may have encountered. We use the term *client* to describe the person or group who is receiving coaching and note in this chapter that the identity of the client is not always obvious. It may be a teacher or leader who is being coached, but there are often other stakeholders who are also part of the clientele the coach must serve. Finally, we consider models of coaching that, despite their labels, are demonstrably ineffective and suggest how the consumers of coaching can separate coaching claims from authentic evidence.

WHAT DOES "COACHING" MEAN, ANYWAY?

The *Wild West* of coaching. The term *coach* has been so broadly applied that it can encompass nearly any relationship in which one person seeks to help another. While coaching has traditionally been associated with the women and men who lead sports teams, the term now encompasses performance enhancement in any field. Coaches of athletic teams have a clear measure of success, the win-loss ratio. This is strongly related to other critical success factors of the team, including ticket sales, advertiser affiliations, and the value of the team brand. But in other realms, the value of coaching is much more ambiguous. There are instructional coaches, leadership coaches, team coaches, life coaches, relationship coaches, personal coaches, accountability coaches, career coaches, executive coaches, strategic coaches, and specialty coaches, to name just a few (Eckfeldt, 2019). The *Harvard Business Review* described the application of coaching to the leaders of business and nonprofit organizations as "the Wild West" in which anyone could call themselves a coach, irrespective of the research, method, and perspective that that self-labeled coach provides. While there are a few coaching relationships in which results can be quantified (MacKie, 2016), the most common indicator of success is the personal satisfaction of the client, rather than the results for the client's organization, which almost always is paying the bill for the coaching. In this book, we are focused on instructional coaching, leadership coaching, and team coaching.

We define clearly what *Fearless Coaching* is and what it is not. Our definition of Fearless Coaching is simple and clear:

> *Fearless Coaching is a process of inquiry, strengths identification, feedback, and mutual accountability in pursuit of client goals and the greater good for students, teachers, leaders, communities, and the educational world.*

This is based on a relationship in which the client, the client's organization, and the coach develop clearly defined goals and regularly monitor progress toward those goals.

In the pages that follow, you will see how this definition of coaching differs markedly from the vast majority of coaching practices. We are not contending that alternative definitions of coaching are bad; rather, we are simply distinguishing the coaching model in this book from the ambiguity and inconsistency that is representative of many coaching approaches.

WHY FEARLESS COACHING IS DIFFERENT

Let us consider each part of the definition of Fearless Coaching: goals, inquiry, strengths, feedback, and accountability. In the Fearless Coaching model, goals include not only those associated with job performance but also include personal and organizational aspirations. We have learned that if the client is struggling with a personal goal (e.g., health, relationships, or personal development), then the emotional and intellectual energy invested in this personal goal will inevitably divert attention from their focus on professional and organizational coaching goals. Therefore, it is essential that the coach is aware of these personal challenges and attentive to the state of mind of the client who is pursuing them.

As James Clear (2018) has noted, goals can be overwhelming unless we break them down into small increments. Whether the goal is losing weight, running a marathon, helping with household chores, or writing an article or book, the role of the coach is not to be the cheerleader at the finish line but to provide feedback at each step along the way. Coaches must, therefore, understand all of the client's goals in order to effectively support the client's growth. To put a fine point on it, the client doesn't need the coach at the 26th mile of the Boston Marathon when the assembled runners complete the race. The client needs the coach at mile 20, where Heartbreak Hill begins and the runners' legs feel as if they are made of rubber, and all of their previous vows to run through the pain have evaporated. The client does not need the coach at the graduation ceremony for the placement of the hood of the newly minted recipient of a doctoral degree. The client needs the coach when the proposal was rejected, the committee required another draft, and the frustrated dissertation writer was ready to quit. The client does not need the coach when students and faculty are cheering at the beginning of school but in the dog-days of winter when attendance is down, failure is up—and faculty, students, and parents are all disengaged from the enterprise of learning. Chapter 14 addresses the leading indicators, the observable practices of teachers and leaders, that are most clearly associated with the educational goals of schools and systems. The heart of effective coaching conversations depends upon a regular consideration, not merely of the results the client is seeking, but of the specific actions the client is taking to achieve those results.

Clients have both personal and organizational goals, and the two are inextricably linked. Personal goals, including professional learning, health, and organization—to name just a few—are vital to the ability of the client to achieve organizational goals. There is an understandable desire of supervisors to stand far off from the personal goals of their subordinates. What if the goals of the client are in conflict with the goals of the organization? Consider these potential conflicts:

- What if my goal for better family relationships means that I can't respond to emails after 6:00 p.m., even though students, parents, and my boss continue to send emails throughout the evening?
- What if my commitment to professional learning includes weekend classes, and I will miss some weekend meetings with district leaders?
- What if my goals include educational advancement and another degree, which may lead to the opportunity to leave the organization?

If the coach only knows about organizational goals without considering personal goals, then it is as if the coach is working with only a puppet, while the real person operating the puppet is hiding behind the curtain. While it may be possible to support the puppet, every observer knows that the interaction between the coach and the puppet is superficial and unhelpful to the puppeteer. The real person—the puppeteer whom the audience does not see—is the person with whom the coach must establish a trusting and fearless relationship.

What Does Success Mean?

There are important similarities between personal and organizational success. At the personal level, if success means reading bedtime stories to my kids, then it is very likely that I will come to work energized rather than embittered. If, at the personal level, it means that my marathon training required missing some Saturday morning meetings, it probably means, at the very least, that my employer's health insurance costs are lower than would have otherwise been the case had I remained sedentary and overweight. At best, it means that my colleagues and supervisors would appreciate the deep intensity, care, and empathy for others that I bring to the workplace. The best marathon pictures are, after all, not those of the person breaking through the finish line alone but the pictures of those who walk, limp, or crawl across the finish line together. There are few better experiences for a leader or team to see than a vision of completing the Marine Corps Marathon in Arlington, Virginia, the last quarter-mile of which is uphill to the Iwo Jima Monument. When the marathon finishers behold the four marines hoisting the American Flag, it's impossible to think about how sore their feet, ankles, and calf muscles may be.

Defining Success

One of the greatest challenges of coaching is defining success. The lowest level of this definition is "customer satisfaction", a friendly relationship between coach and client. This is a quality that depends upon a sympathetic and fawning personal relationship. If the fundamental element of coaching is constructive change, then we must recognize that change requires pain, the release of past convictions and firmly held beliefs and practices. The coach who is supporting this change is required to challenge past practices, and that is not the basis of a warm and fuzzy friendship.

Change requires the replacement of a past orientation with a future orientation and requires a step into the unknown. This requires risk and occasional failure, and the coach who encourages risk-taking and the failure that goes with it will not always be popular with the client. Coaches will find that affirming the past will engender much higher ratings than exploring the future. The unknown is scary, uncertain, and full of fear. Reliving the past is safe, known, and full of personal satisfaction. Who could blame the client for preferring a focus on the past? Fearless Coaching requires this fundamental challenge: Will you focus on the past or on the future? We do not ignore the past, including successes and failures, but we must not be obsessed by it.

Leadership Leverage

A cardinal principle of Fearless Coaching is leverage. While many organizations pride themselves on an exclusive focus on results, we find that this is a short-sighted and potentially counterproductive way of thinking. A focus on results, without an equivalent focus on the leadership actions that caused those results, has two harmful effects. First, ignorance of the causes of results prevents individual and organizational learning. It is the circular reasoning of many educational accountability systems in which the question is, "How do I get higher scores?" The answer, of course, is—be a better teacher. Then we ask, "How do I become a better teacher?" And the *unhelpful* answer is—have higher scores. The waste of energy in this circular reasoning is not the worst impact of an exclusive focus on results. Consider the goal of reducing the obesity crisis in the United States. Obesity rates rose from 30.5% in 2000 to 42.4 % in 2020 (Centers for Disease Control and Prevention, 2020). Obesity is related to a variety of serious medical conditions, including stroke, heart disease, diabetes, and cancer. The cost of obesity, largely born by taxpayers, is an estimated $147 billion. So if you were an obesity coach, then one could hardly blame you for focusing on results, weighing your clients every day and plotting their progress. But if you did not monitor the causes of changes in weight of your clients, you would never know whether weight loss ("progress", in the context of obesity) was related to diet and exercise, or to anorexia and drug abuse. After all, the only thing that matters is results, right?

The Learning Imperative

The essential coaching question is not simply how did my client change? Rather, it is what did my client learn about the process of change? Note well that this is not about the coach teaching the client, as if the coach were simply an instructor on the art of change. Oscar Wilde famously noted that, "Nothing worth knowing can be taught." (Duenning, 2018). This is not to disparage teachers but to challenge the notion that teaching through the delivery of information alone is sufficient for deep learning. Wilde's aphorism is supported by evidence that we learn from experiences and reflection far more than we learn from lectures (Reuell, 2019). I confess that I like lectures and enjoy the intellectual stimulation of a great teacher. The Harvard study found that students also prefer a great lecture to the more challenging task of engaging in experiences. But the evidence is clear—we learn by doing, not by mere listening. Therefore, the job of the coach is never to lecture but to engage in a process of inquiry that leads the client to action. It is the lessons learned from these actions that best serve the client.

Leadership versus Management—the False Dichotomy

Since the seminal *Harvard Business Review* article "Leaders and Managers: Are They Different?" (Zaleznik, 1992), people in organizations have been careful to distinguish their roles. Managers, after all, are the hapless schleps who just provide a safe and secure environment; ensure that curriculum, instruction, and assessment are aligned; and get people paid on time. Leaders, by contrast, think great thoughts and produce grand visions. Among the many bilious statements about managers and leaders is that leaders do the right things, while managers merely do things right. The late Warren Bennis, who popularized this distinction, also contended:

- The manager relies on control; the leader inspires trust.
- The manager is a copy; the leader is an original.
- The manager accepts the status quo; the leader challenges it. (Boynton, 2016)

While Bennis—whose experience was as a university president, leadership scholar, and global leadership guru—was right in many things, I think his emphasis on the leadership-management dichotomy is wrong. In the 21st century, it is not possible to be a great leader without also mastering fundamental management skills. These include managing time, projects, people, money, and technology. Moreover, managers who attend to the details of these areas must also not merely "do things right"; they must, as leaders do, challenge the status quo, inspire trust, and bring innovation and creativity to their jobs every day. In an environment in which technology can be overwhelming, leaders must have the discipline—the management discipline—to focus their time and energy and the resources of the organizations they lead on what matters most. Unfortunately, the vast majority of leaders do not lead professional lives of focus but are fragmented into disconnected priorities that lead to organizational confusion and ambiguity (Newport, 2016).

Therefore, Fearless Coaches must ask blunt questions about how the leader allocates time and attention. When the typical explanation for not achieving goals is, "I just don't have the time!" the coach must respectfully challenge that statement as fundamentally false. The truth is that we all have the same amount of time: 24 hours a day, 7 days a week. The challenge is not the lack of time but a lack of focus, coupled with the unwillingness to challenge traditional norms about how leaders should spend their time. Organizational drag, often associated with wasteful and unnecessary meetings, colleagues who are in the wrong position, and the chronic fatigue of leaders, can incur multi-billions in costs for organizations of all types (Mankins & Garton, 2017). While the leader is thinking great thoughts, someone needs to manage the most precious resource the leader has—her time. And the best person to do that is the leader herself. She can, for example, dramatically improve the way that meetings are conducted and, for that matter, whether they should be held in the first place (Rogelberg, 2019; Reeves, 2020c).

Moreover, the leader can dramatically improve organizational communication and coherence by stopping the wasteful tradition of instant responses to emails, texts, and the other barrage of diversions that prevent staff members from focusing on their greatest priority—student learning. Knowledge workers—who are the people reading this book—check email on average every six minutes, and it can take more than 20 minutes to return to fully focused attention on the task that was the priority before email and texts derailed the attentional train (Hari, 2022).

DEFINING THE REAL CLIENT

In any coaching relationship, it is essential that the coach and client understand who the real client is. In some cases, such as when the client is personally paying for the services of the coach, the answer is easy. The client is the person being coached. But in the vast majority of coaching relationships, defining the real client is more complicated. It might be the Human Resources department that regards leadership coaching as part of their talent development portfolio. It could be senior leaders in the organization who expect the coach to improve the performance of a subordinate. It could be the governing board that is providing executive coaching to senior leaders. In these complex and common coaching relationships, the parties must have clear ground rules about what is confidential and what is not. For example, performance on organizational goals must be transparent, so that everyone in the organization sees not only the progress toward the goals but also how the client is making progress. But most coaching relationships also include personal goals that may be related to organizational goals but are intensely private. To have a trusting relationship, the coach must be clear at the beginning about what parts of the coaching conversations can be disclosed and what must remain private.

Effective coaching relationships include a focus on personal and organizational accountability. This includes actions to which the client committed as well as organizational support that the client seeks or directs. If, for example, the client requires greater focus, then the coach can identify some specific commitments, such as a day every month for focused thinking, or 45 minutes of uninterrupted think-time for deep work twice a week (Newport, 2016). These are clear and specific goals directly related to the success of the leader, and goals for which accountability is very specific. The time is either clearly allocated on the leader's calendar or it isn't. Productivity expert and Georgetown computer science professor Cal Newport notes that the calendar reflects the priorities of the leader. He recommends time-block planning in which serious chunks of time are set aside for uninterrupted work on the leader's greatest priorities (Newport, 2021). If the leader's calendar consists primarily of meetings and events, then it is clear that the serious work of thinking through and achieving goals is a mere afterthought.

The tendency of many leaders is to set too many goals, rendering accountability conversations nearly impossible. My own research and that of other scholars suggests the Rule of Six, in which it is not possible for a leader to focus on more than six priorities at one time (Reeves, 2021a). One of the greatest contributions a Fearless Coach can make to the client is not the addition of new things to accomplish; rather, it is to assist the client to evaluate critically the things that are burying the client under a sea of initiatives. By creating a "not-to-do" list, the coach will help the client focus on what matters most. Before new medical programs are begun, physicians and hospitals must engage in a process of "de-implementation", which means that you can't start a new pharmaceutical or surgical treatment without stopping previous treatments (Hamilton, et. al., 2022). In education, by contrast, the more common practice is to pile one program on top of another, guaranteeing fragmented leadership attention and very frustrated teachers.

A critical coaching question is: What barriers are stopping you from achieving your goals? In many cases, the barriers are external: technology, money, and people lead the list. But many barriers are internal—choices within the control of the client about what meetings to attend, how to organize the day, and how to invest time. One of my coaches asked me a very pointed question: "For the past three sessions you have been talking about the same person as a barrier to achieving your goals. How is today going to be different?" With those words, my coach earned her fee. Even though I coach others and consider myself well-informed on the subject, I must regularly confront that question: "How is today going to be different?" The barriers to change fall into three categories: factors we can control, factors we can influence but not control, and factors that we can neither influence nor control. By labeling each barrier into one of these three categories, we can let go of the last category—factors we can neither influence nor control—and focus on the first two categories.

This perspective is especially important in coaching classroom teachers. Without this focus, it is too tempting to lose precious time in collaborative teams about matters we can neither influence nor control. We can redirect emotional and intellectual energy away from things like the state of the global economy and focus instead on the factors we can control, the daily decisions we make in allocation of time and energy. We also recognize that there are factors influencing the performance of our colleagues that we cannot control—their personal lives, financial distress, and illnesses. While leaders must be empathetic with these factors and exercise appropriate care for their colleagues, they must focus their time and energy on the factors they can control—the skills the colleague needs to develop and the way that they apply those skills.

HOW TO IDENTIFY AND AVOID INEFFECTIVE MODELS OF COACHING

Mentor: Named for the wise elder who guided Odysseus, the coach as mentor offers guidance and advice. While this model seems appealing, it exemplifies the difference that Fearless Coaching represents. While the mentor makes wise statements, the most effective coaches ask questions. The mentor reveals wisdom based on the experience of the mentor. The coach reveals wisdom based on the experiences and insights of the client.

Consultant: The old joke is that the consultant steals your watch and then charges you to tell the time. If it were that simple, then the major consultancies such as McKinsey and Bain would not exist. At their best, consultants organize information, frame problems, and offer solutions. Clients are often overwhelmed by their own data. An effective consultant can help analyze that data in a way that helps the client challenge prevailing assumptions. For example, in the field of education, people often assume that the causes of student failure are a combination of poor attendance and bad behavior. This impression prevails because the image of the misbehaving student is very vivid and front of mind for many teachers and school administrators. The data, however, may tell a different story. While attendance and behavior are important, what are the alternative hypotheses that explain student failure? The effective consultant will sift through the data and find examples of students with 90% or greater attendance and no disciplinary infractions, who nevertheless are failing. This provides a different perspective on the client's own data and challenges prevailing wisdom.

There are many other examples, however, of consultants who simply apply their own tools to every client problem. When the only tool you have is a hammer, then every problem looks like a nail. We have seen, for example, consultants who have expertise in a particular software platform, such as Salesforce, and apply that platform to every problem, including those that are far afield from the customer relations management problems for which Salesforce was designed. Moreover, when consultants have expertise in reorganization or re-engineering, then they can justify their fees based on cost savings that are almost always associated with eliminating employee positions. It is entirely possible that these cost reductions are justified, but it is equally possible that *reorganization* becomes a synonym for a fear-based organization in which trust, confidence, and focus on priorities are displaced by suspicion and fear. The evidence is overwhelming that, especially in an educational environment, fear is the enemy of learning (Edmondson, 2018).

Therapist: There is nothing wrong with therapy, especially therapeutic approaches that have solid scientific backing, such as Cognitive Behavioral Therapy (Clancy, 2020). However, many people holding themselves out to be executive coaches are essentially practicing therapy without the burden of becoming a licensed psychotherapist. They listen, reflect, and mimic the therapists they have seen in movies and television shows with phrases such as, "What I hear you saying is ____." Most of all, they seek to offer the clients reassurance and to massage their egos. This is not coaching, and it's probably not good therapy.

Evaluator: One of the worst abuses of coaching is the engagement of a coach to evaluate the client. This unfortunate tactic occurs when an organization has determined that an employee should be terminated, but lacking sufficient grounds to fire the employee, the employer seeks to have outside affirmation of the decision. The "coach" is not there to build individual and organizational capacity but simply to interrogate the employee and justify the decision of the organization. "We gave him every chance," the organizational leader can rationalize, "and we even offered him an executive coach! When that didn't work, we decided that he had to go." This is disingenuous, and whatever this person who engages in the practice may be, the last label that should be applied to the activity is *coaching*. I have never seen anyone be "evaluated into better performance", but I have seen many educators and leaders improve performance through nonevaluative coaching.

* * *

In the next chapter we will explore the biggest coaching mistakes and how to avoid them.

QUESTIONS FOR REFLECTION:

1. Have you had both a mentor and a coach? How were the roles different?
2. Looking back, how would you have personally or professionally benefited from a coach?
3. How can an organization benefit from coaches?
4. Think of a leader with whom you have worked, or reflect on your own leadership experience. What are the most powerful leadership levers that you have observed?
5. After processing Chapter 1, how will today be different?

CHAPTER 2

THE ELEVEN BIGGEST COACHING MISTAKES: AND HOW TO AVOID THEM

- ❖ Coach Fails to Establish Trust with Client
- ❖ Coach Fails to Define and Stick to Roles of Coach and Client
- ❖ Coach Allows Talk as a Substitute for Action
- ❖ Coach and Client Fail to Define Success in Clear and Measurable Terms
- ❖ Coach Uses Friendship as a Barrier to Candid Feedback
- ❖ Coaching Conversations Focus on Uncontrollable Factors
- ❖ Coach Fails to Understand Personal and Family Crises of Client
- ❖ Coach Uses "Smart Talk" to Avoid Discussing Essential Issues
- ❖ Coach Serves as Expert and Consultant, Rather Than Challenging Clients to Build Their Own Expertise
- ❖ Coach Is Not Prepared for the Session
- ❖ Coach and Client Fail to Make Their Meetings "Sacred Time"

COACH FAILS TO ESTABLISH TRUST WITH CLIENT

Trust is at the center of any relationship. This is especially true in the context of Fearless Coaching, in which a key ingredient of the coaching relationship is the willingness of the client to admit mistakes, learn from them, and at the highest level, help other parts of the organization learn from those mistakes as well. Yet in organizational life, too many coaches try to build trust with what some researchers call the "Resumé Approach" (Snow, 2020). These coaches seek to establish their trustworthiness based on their degrees, qualifications, and experience. However impressive those credentials may be, they are not remotely close to the essence of trust, and their existence does not prove that the coach cares about the client as a person.

In their landmark study of trusting organizations, Kouzes and Posner (2011) found that leaders can flounder in many areas of competence but be forgiven by their colleagues for it if they are trusted; however, once they lack credibility, no amount of technical or managerial skill can make up for the lack of trust. Their simple formulation is that trustworthy people do what they say they will do. When they agree to a deadline, they either meet or negotiate an extension well before the deadline date arrives. If they agree to keep something confidential, they do so absolutely. Interestingly, this promise of confidentiality can irritate some clients, such as when they ask a coach about another client. Once the coach steps across that boundary, then the Rubicon has been crossed and there is little ability to gain back that credibility. Therefore, trust is not the result of a feeling or impression but the result of action. Early in the relationship, the coach must make commitments and, without fail, keep them.

COACH FAILS TO DEFINE AND STICK TO ROLES OF COACH AND CLIENT

The first coaching session began with the following uncomfortable question from the client: "Just how bad is my performance that my boss thinks I need a coach? I've seen this play before, and coaching is what HR does when they want to be able to say that they have provided all the support they could before they fired somebody." This skepticism is completely understandable, as coaching has often been misused for evaluation or the illusion of support. The Fearless Coach will seize this opportunity to make the roles of the coach and client clear. Therefore, the coach might respond, "I completely understand your concerns. It's true that coaching has been misused in the past in many organizations, but Fearless Coaching is different. The coach is not an evaluator. Rather, the coach is here to identify and build on your strengths and help you be as successful as you want to be. Unless you put someone at risk or behave in an illegal manner, our conversations are confidential, and I won't share anything about our discussions and my observations unless you give me permission to do so. So let's do a reset in this conversation so that we get off to a good start. Will that work for you?"

COACH ALLOWS TALK AS A SUBSTITUTE FOR ACTION

My former executive coach was a person of genuine warmth and steely resolve all wrapped into a very powerful set of skills with which she both led her own international organization and also provided coaching to a few clients. Many clients, including me, are steeped in the literature of success, leadership, and coaching. We can talk the talk and never fail to substitute an indecipherable acronym or a multisyllabic word when plain speaking might have served us better. We can, as my coach said, "admire the problem," without taking the concrete steps necessary to address it. The Fearless Coach will help the client break a challenge down into its component parts and then ask the central question, "What can you do now—today—to make progress on this one small part of the challenge you are facing?"

The central goal of Fearless Coaching, in sum, is not merely to describe and admire problems until our vocal cords are strained but to take concrete steps every day to achieve the goal. This is almost always a combination of removing barriers and taking direct steps for goal achievement. One of the most common subjects of coaching conversations is the disappointment of the leader in the performance of colleagues. When we ask leaders, "What was the response of your colleague when you told him about your concerns?"—the answer in most cases is that the clients have not discussed their disappointments with their colleagues. On the contrary, many of these leaders see their role as cheerleaders who celebrate a goal before the game has begun. They fear that honest conversation will imperil their relationships with colleagues, not recognizing that almost everyone in the organization wishes that they had more frequent, specific, and constructive feedback. The yawning gaps between performance reviews allow every person in the organization to fill in the vacuum of feedback with their worst fears.

While objective performance goals can be monitored by the employee with the oversight of a manager, one of the most time-consuming and futile tasks of management is to evaluate employees on their performance and potential. There is scant evidence that these typical evaluations are anything more than a colossal waste of time and resources (Buckingham & Goodall, 2019). Their self-talk becomes a greater burden than the projects on which they must make progress. The leader who offers to move a deadline based upon the workflow of the organization is interpreted by subordinates as, "She knows I missed a deadline and she thinks I'm incompetent." Productivity is replaced by paralyzing fear. And fearfulness in any organization is deadly.

This claim is not hyperbole, as Harvard Professor Amy Edmondson makes clear (Edmondson, 2018). When people are fearful, they cover up mistakes, ensuring that organizational learning does not take place. In the hospitals that Edmondson studied, the result was that medical teams operating in fear would see mistakes and rarely address them, ensuring that organizational learning never occurred. But in the atmosphere of psychological safety, medical staff would feel safe to challenge one another in the interest of patient safety, learn together, and know that every mistake, when publicly shared and used as a springboard for learning, was not a source of shame but a reflection of personal and professional courage. The same is true in schools, where learning flourishes only when leaders and educators confidently share their successes and their failures (Reeves, 2021b).

Perhaps the worst example of talk as a substitute for action is the proliferation of email. Georgetown computer science professor Cal Newport (2021) amassed a mountain of evidence that—far from improving productivity and communication—most emails have a counterproductive impact on performance. With the average employee checking email every six minutes and clinging to their electronic devices from the time they awake until the minute their weary head hits the pillow, the opportunity for substantive collaboration and the application of focused thinking on cognitively demanding tasks evaporates. While some people may think that email saves time compared to a phone call or face-to-face conversation, the opposite is true. Email has no emotional context, so that the same words conveyed in an email have significantly more opportunities for a negative and accusatory tone than is the case when people have interpersonal contact.

COACH AND CLIENT FAIL TO DEFINE SUCCESS IN CLEAR AND MEASURABLE TERMS

Almost everyone has heard of SMART Goals. Depending on which version of goal-setting guidelines you are reading, the elements of the acronym vary, but they often are associated with the following:

- Specific
- Measurable
- Achievable
- Relevant
- Time-bound

The elements of SMART goals are hard to argue with because they make intuitive sense, but as I reviewed more than 2,000 school plans, the central question was this: To what degree, if any, do the requirements of the plan's content relate to the achievement of the plan's goals? It turned out that the key elements of SMART goals were specificity and measurability (D. Reeves, 2016). While the other elements of these goals may be useful, the research suggested that it was the first two elements of SMART goals that were most related to desired results. In coaching conversations, the question is never: Did you fill out the form correctly? Rather, it is: How do you know that your leadership actions are related to your desired goals?

One of the clearest ways for the coach and client to focus on the most important results is the process of Objectives and Key Results (OKR), pioneered in Silicon Valley but now used in organizations of every size around the world (Doerr, 2018). Unlike the goal tracking programs of byzantine complexity, OKRs focus the individual, team, and entire organization on what matters most. Moreover, this process focuses on causes—not just results. When the client focuses only on results, it makes it impossible to understand how to replicate and improve those results. Moreover, when the client focuses only on causes, always busy and always doing what he believes to be important, there is no opportunity to understand if all that work is, well, working.

A note of caution with respect to the goals of the client. While most educational leaders focus on state test scores, it is essential that clients have short-term goals including both student performance and the specific actions of teachers and school leaders. For example, if the goal is attainment of an A-rating by a state department of education, then the Fearless Coach must ask the client, "What do you need to do in the next thirty days to move toward that goal?"

Short-term goals that lead to long-term success might include, for example, a commitment by the school leader to provide feedback based on ten-minute mini-observations to 100% of teachers within 30 days, using the rubrics in the appendices to this book. "I will have 100% engagement from students every day for the next month," along with a commitment to post the percentage of engagement at the end of each month. The teachers might also have a goal regarding how they will achieve 100% engagement, such as the use of equity sticks, so that 100% of students have an equal opportunity to be called on to participate in class.

COACH USES FRIENDSHIP AS A BARRIER TO CANDID FEEDBACK

Friends don't let friends do dumb things. At the very least, they try to persuade them to avoid calamity. This is the difference between the cheerleader, who never saw a client's misguided idea that the coach did not applaud, and the Fearless Coach, who is willing to politely but relentlessly challenge the client. One of the central challenges for clients is not to confuse attentive listening with approval. The coach can use encouraging phrases such as, "I'd like to learn more about your perspective on this" and "Please help me understand how you have come to this conclusion" without signaling agreement.

The ability to challenge beliefs, attitudes, and actions that are unsupported by the evidence is an essential attribute of the effective coach. Consider the example of the learning styles theory, in which children are labeled as visual, auditory, or kinesthetic learners. After this diagnosis, teachers are then expected to adapt their teaching to the learning style of the student. University of Virginia cognitive scientist Daniel Willingham (2021) notes that, while more than 80% of teachers believe in learning styles theory, a voluminous body of evidence has led him to conclude that learning-styles theory is simply wrong. The theory survives on what Willingham describes as social evidence, distinguished more by popularity than by rigorous examination. While it might be tempting to simply let this matter slide and avoid a difficult conversation with the client, Fearless Coaching demands mutual respect and a commitment to students. And it is fundamentally disrespectful if the coach fails to address professional practices that are wrong. The greatest challenge for every teacher is time, and every moment devoted to specious theories and ineffective practices is a moment that could be devoted to exceptional practices that lead to better student learning, effective teaching, and sound leadership.

COACHING CONVERSATIONS FOCUS ON UNCONTROLLABLE FACTORS

There are three inboxes—virtual or physical—on every client's desk. The first inbox is full of factors that she cannot control. That includes external factors such as the socioeconomic status of students, the structure of families, and the weather. The coach and client can consider how to react to those conditions, but they cannot influence or control those factors, and to perseverate about them is a waste of valuable time.

The second inbox includes factors that the client can influence but not control. School leaders, for example, can influence attendance and on-time arrivals at school, but they cannot control those factors. Some leaders insist that they only help students once they arrive in school, and it is not possible to influence whether the students show up or the degree to which they arrive on time. But the way we know that this influence is possible is an examination of dramatic improvements in attendance in the same school with the same families and the same schedule. When, for example, attendance in schools in Greenfield, Wisconsin, and Newark, New Jersey, improved from 50% in the days of September 2020—the depth of the global pandemic—to 97–99% in the spring of 2021, these dramatic changes were the result of decisive action and persistent communication for leaders and staff members.

One of the key skills of the coach is root-cause analysis. The third inbox focuses exclusively on the factors that the client can control—that is, the client's actions, decisions, and communications. Coaches are most helpful when they help the client focus on this third inbox.

COACH FAILS TO UNDERSTAND PERSONAL AND FAMILY CRISES OF CLIENT

Coaching is complex because it requires an understanding of the whole client, not just their performance at work, but also the context of the client outside of work. While it is important to respect the privacy of the client, very early in the relationship the coach should ask about family, interests outside of work, the client's pursuit of an advanced degree, and stressors outside of work. If the client is distracted by a personal or family crisis, the coach has the opportunity to better understand the client and also serve as an advocate. While many high-performing leaders have taken pride in "playing hurt", they soon learn that heroism may get accolades in the short term, but it is not a sustainable strategy. From the myths of the ancient Greeks to the news reports of the 21st century, high-flying heroes may enjoy a moment in the sun, but they ultimately burn out. One of the causes of this may be overload at work, but another likely cause is the failure to understand the client's life outside of the office. If, for example, the client is caring for a newborn or has a child in the hospital, restorative sleep is rare. Sleep deprivation takes a toll on concentration and focus and adversely affects the health of the client (*Sleep and Mental Health*, n.d.). While this client might claim that she can power through any obstacle and appears unphased by these family challenges, the wise coach will ask how some of her duties can be delegated and also explain how her performance on her highest priorities could be improved with better health and more sleep.

Although the coach should never pretend to be a therapist or serve in the role of a mental health counselor, the coach can certainly ask the client about the availability of employee assistance programs (EAP) that many organizations have. These programs provide support for a wide variety of issues, including depression, stress, anxiety, and substance abuse. The failure to take advantage of these services when needed hurts not only the client but also the entire organization (Leslie, 2021).

COACH USES "SMART TALK" TO AVOID DISCUSSING ESSENTIAL ISSUES

In our observations of the interactions between coaches and clients around the world, their discussions can quickly be divided into two categories: philosophy and practice. While it is true that educational philosophy can form the foundation on which teaching and leadership depend, discussions about educational philosophy that fail to include specific implications for teachers and leaders are vapid exchanges of opinions that are redolent of sophomoric debates about the meaning of life. For example, most educators and leaders are committed to the principle of equity. Few people would disagree about the value of equity. However, conversations about equity that fail to address the practices and policies that undermine equity are disingenuous (Collado, 2021). Too many equity conversations are focused on guilt and public apologies (DiAngelo & Dyson, 2018) rather than on the central question of how to address structural inequities in the classroom. This occurs daily when educators and leaders are required to attend workshops and speeches about equity but are permitted to maintain professional practices that are persistently inequitable, such as toxic grading policies.

COACH SERVES AS EXPERT CONSULTANT, RATHER THAN CHALLENGING CLIENTS TO BUILD THEIR OWN EXPERTISE

It is common that the same person is sometimes a coach and sometimes a client. Although the person may be the same, their functions are quite different. The essence of the difference is this: Coaches ask questions, consultants give answers. Clients hire consultants to address a specific need, such as installing new software, conducting equity training, or analyzing financial results. Consultants provide specific expertise that the client does not have and probably will not create internally. Therefore, the consultant, by definition, is not seeking to create internal capacity but only to provide an answer to meet short-term needs. In other cases, the consultant is hired to provide an external and objective voice to address a particularly thorny issue, such as the performance of a team or a leader, or how to evaluate that performance.

The coach, by contrast, seeks to create capacity for the client and for the client's organization. This means that the effective coach will not say: promote this person, or buy this software, or break up this team. Rather, the coach asks, "Please tell me what you know about the performance of the person you are considering promoting. What data do you have to support this decision? Who is at least one other candidate for promotion?" While the coach does not provide answers about finances or software, the effective coach can ask essential questions, such as, "What decisions have you made in the past about finances and software? Which decisions turned out best and which had bad results? Why do you think that is?"

The reason that this line of questioning is so important is the results fallacy, the assumption that good results always spring from good decisions and that bad results spring from bad decisions. While many leaders like to think of their executive decision-making as a game of chess, a better analogy is poker (Konnikova, 2020). Why? In chess, there is theoretically always one best answer for every move. That's why the IBM computer Big Blue was able to beat grand masters. By contrast, poker combines strategy and chance. In chess, every piece is clearly displayed on the board—there are no unknown variables. But in leadership decisions, there are always unknown variables that are beyond the control of the leader. Therefore, an excellent strategy can, with bad luck, yield bad results. A terrible and impulsive strategy—the prototypical gut-level decisions that are unburdened by evidence and careful thought—can yield great results, not because of the intuitive genius of the leader but because of her good fortune.

This is why it is imperative that the coach is focused not merely on results but on the relationship between strategy and chance. The coach will temper the self-criticism of the leader who, after executing a flawless strategy, saw poor results. In education, poor results may stem from inferior leadership and teaching, or because a high transiency rate of students prevented the school from having a positive impact on learning. It's difficult to teach students to prepare for end-of-year tests when they arrive in the seventh month of a nine-month school year. The coach might also temper the self-congratulation of the leaders who, despite failures in teacher observation, curriculum, and assessment, nevertheless see "gains" in performance due to a redistricting that brought in affluent students to the school who were reading before they entered kindergarten. In the latter case, it is easy for the leader—and some of the students—to think that because they were born on third base, they hit a triple.

COACH IS NOT PREPARED FOR THE SESSION

Imagine that you are seeking the advice of a physician for lower back pain. You have already had X-rays and MRIs, you have spoken to nurses and a physician's assistant to describe your symptoms, and you have filled out multipage forms in order to finally see the doctor. At last, you will see the doctor and, dressed in a gown that leaves little room for modesty, you are seated on the examination table. Despite all of this prior preparation, the physician enters the room and asks, "What brings you in today?" Frustrated? That is precisely how clients feel when, after having published their goals, values, plans, and achievement data on their web site, the coach has ignored all of the available information and asks, "What brings you in today?"

Clients have the right to expect that coaches have done their homework. Sometimes this will accelerate the conversation between client and coach. Other times, however, the client might say, "That stuff is still on our website? That was five years and two superintendents ago and none of it applies to what we are doing today." Whether or not the information that the coach has gleaned prior to the client engagement meeting is relevant, the essential lesson is that Fearless Coaches do their homework. If the publicly available information is useful, then the coach can get a head start in essential conversations. If the information is not accurate, then this presents an opportunity for the coach and client to address why inaccurate and outdated information is being distributed to the public.

What information does the coach need? A partial list of what the coach should examine before the first meeting includes the following:

- District mission, vision, and values
- School mission, vision, and values
- District strategic plan
- School improvement plan
- Surveys of key stakeholders—teachers, students, parents, and community
- School and district performance data for the past three years
- School and district protocols for reviewing and analyzing data

This list is a good start, and many schools and districts may have more information. My experience is that even on the basic issues of mission, vision, and values, very few clients can recite this information without referring to a poster or cleverly designed card printed with the intention that every administrator and teacher will have the words of the mission, vision, and values imprinted on their memory. In the first meeting, the coach and client must acknowledge that chasm between rhetoric and reality. The soaring rhetoric may be about preparing children to be global leaders in the 21st century, but the reality may be that the client must hire three teachers, a bus driver, and a special education paraprofessional before sundown.

In the frenetic world of clients, there is little time for philosophy, as they must focus on the crises of the moment. Only when the coach recognizes the complex reality of the client can an authentic and trusting relationship be established between the coach and client.

COACH AND CLIENT FAIL TO MAKE THEIR MEETINGS "SACRED TIME"

One of the most important early commitments that coaches and clients must achieve is the value of time. The coach can, for example, give the client a choice about the time of coaching meetings. "Which is better for you—a monthly block of fifty minutes, or two separate twenty-five-minute meetings?" This simple offer can overcome the reality that teachers and leaders rarely have 50 uninterrupted minutes during the workday. Some clients prefer early-morning meetings before students arrive, and others prefer late in the day. A few might prefer weekends or evenings. Whatever the ultimate time commitment, the client and coach must agree that this is sacred time. This is the time to eliminate all other distractions—no phones, no texts, no emails, no interruptions—just a solid commitment of time for intense and focused conversation between client and coach. It is possible that there are exceptions to this rule of focus, such as when the client or client's spouse goes into labor or when there is a genuine emergency that demands the attention of the client. But aside from those emergencies, the coach and client must be able to commit to one another the gift of focus.

* * *

In this chapter we considered eleven essential coaching mistakes and how to anticipate and avoid them. In the next chapter we will carefully examine the coach-client relationship.

QUESTIONS FOR REFLECTION:

1. In your experience as a coach or a person receiving coaching, what are the avoidable mistakes you have seen? How could those mistakes have been avoided?
2. Imagine a situation in which your coaching clients are clearly preoccupied. They are multitasking; you can see their eyes averted in many different directions on the screen. They have difficulty following the thread of the conversation. They are unprepared for the coaching session. How would you react? What are the exact words you would use to learn about the client's needs in the moment?
3. Your coaching client begins every meeting with a series of complaints about student poverty, parental neglect, chronic absenteeism, and other factors that preoccupy the client every day. As a Fearless Coach, what questions will you ask the client in order to guide the conversation in a manner that is most productive and helpful?

CHAPTER 3
THE COACH-CLIENT RELATIONSHIP

- ❖ Coach Is on the Sidelines, Not in the Game
- ❖ Coach Notices What Works and What Doesn't
- ❖ Coach Is Not Invested in Past Practices and Methods
- ❖ Coach Provides Immediate Clear and Actionable Feedback
- ❖ Coach Listens to All of the Players, Not Just the Team Captain
- ❖ Coach Is Relentlessly Goal-Focused, Linking Actions to Results

COACH IS ON THE SIDELINES, NOT IN THE GAME

IN THE WORLD OF SPORTS, THE COACH IS OFTEN A FLAMBOYANT figure, with only a few millimeters separating them from the field of play. With great dramatic effect, the coach will sometimes rush onto the field to vigorously argue a call by the official. Although improving technology, including instant replays, has reduced errors by officials, it is unlikely that improved officiating will dull the enthusiasm of coaches for ostentatious displays of anger and outrage

(Klapisch, 2019). While these arguments sometimes delight the fans, albeit setting a bit of a bad example of sportsmanship for children watching the game, one thing remains certain: The coach doesn't get to play the game but must influence results by influencing others. The "player-coach" has been, with a few exceptions, a consistent failure in sports and in other organizations. The great salesperson does not always make a great sales manager. The eloquent senator doesn't always make an effective executive, and the most winsome, creative, and empathetic teacher may or may not make a good school administrator.

While it is certainly appropriate for administrators to show that they still have their instructional chops by teaching a class now and then, it undermines the capacity of the classroom teachers when the principal or other outsiders routinely interrupt in an attempt to "help" the teacher. There are, of course, exceptions, such as when the teacher has lost control of the classroom or is engaging in practices that are dangerous or risky. But the most effective coaching engagements do not have the instructional coach taking the place of the teacher or the leadership coach running a staff or cabinet meeting. Rather, the coach is in the background, providing clarity, focus, support, and feedback.

Perhaps the best example of separating the coach from the field of play is Australian Rules Football, or *footie* to its fans. The coach is required to sit in an enclosed glass box in the stands, far from the sidelines, and may only communicate with players through written instructions sent by runners. The team can be penalized if the coach is too involved in playing the game. Thus, the footie coach, like a successful Fearless Coach, supports the client before and after the game in which the leader is involved—but not during the game. To be clear, the coach is not merely a passive observer; coaches can and should interact with students, asking them what they are learning, why they are learning it, and how they will know if they are successful. But the coach does not disrupt the class or divert attention away from the classroom teacher.

COACH NOTICES WHAT WORKS AND WHAT DOESN'T

Leaders are understandably invested in their strategies, plans, and practices. Even in the face of evidence that those practices are not working as planned, we are frequently guilty of what Nobel Prize winner Daniel Kahneman (2013) calls the sunk cost fallacy. This phenomenon is played out in daily life when investors watch a stock drop in value but refuse to sell because only upon a sale will they really lose their money. Based on this erroneous belief, the investor continues to hold stocks long after they should have been sold. We see this in education on a daily basis when a technology program, curriculum, or instructional practice is clearly ineffective, and yet leaders hang on to them because, after all, they already have invested money, time, and prestige in them.

If the leader pulls the plug on a practice or product about which they had been wildly enthusiastic just a few years before, then they might appear weak or incompetent. Better to let the children and teachers suffer through another year of futility rather than losing face. In my own observations of technology programs—particularly those that depend upon the teachers entering data manually on a regular basis—the evidence may be clear that only a tiny fraction of the program is being used as planned. The impact, therefore, is either zero or actually negative, because teacher and administrator time that could have been devoted to effective practice is devoted to the dogged pursuit of ineffective practice and worthless data entry. Nevertheless, someone, typically the person who advocated for the purchase in the past, will insist, "but we really *need* this program!"

It is important to note that the coach need not be an expert in technology or other areas that are vexing a client. Rather, the coach's job is to notice, in as objective a way possible, what is working, what is not, and the consistent challenges that bedevil the client.

COACH IS NOT INVESTED IN PAST PRACTICES AND METHODS

One reason the Fearless Coach can offer objective analysis is that the coach has no vested interest in past practices and methods. The coach can ask naïve questions, such as, "Why do we have this time/expense-consuming meeting every Wednesday?" Or, "Why are half the participants sitting in this meeting not necessarily considering the agenda items that are discussed?" The most common answer, with respect to meetings, is simply *tradition*. In their brilliant book *Time, Talent, Energy* (Mankins & Garton, 2017), the authors ask who in the organization has the authority to spend a million dollars. Usually, the answer is a very senior person, or perhaps the governing board. But when one considers that each meeting among senior staff people results in a cascade of other meetings to send the message along, that first meeting—perhaps scheduled by a new administrative assistant—goes from being a costly waste of time as a single meeting to a million-dollar sinkhole because of all the other meetings that the first meeting generates.

Meetings are not the only instance in which tradition takes precedence over sound judgment. Consider the decision-making process in most schools and districts. At a school, some teachers will explore an idea, perhaps one that they heard at a conference or learned about in their professional reading, and suggest that the principal adopt that for the entire building. At the central office level, critical decisions, including the selection of leaders, purchase of technology, or recommendations for policies are often discussed by staff members who then come to the superintendent or governing board with the best option.

Such a decision-making practice seems sound, as it appears to reflect the best thinking of the professional staff of teachers and central-office administrators. But this single-option, take-it-or-leave-it practice of decision-making is in fact terrible, because it fails to explore other alternatives. There is never a perfect decision option, and every decision alternative has advantages and disadvantages. But our discomfort with competition, with winners and losers at the table, pushes dissent into the background. This is especially true on complex decisions where a single person or small group may have a monopoly on expertise. And it is especially true of technology, assessment, and financial decisions, where the loudest voice may not be the most informed voice (Reeves, 2020c).

In order to have better decisions, leaders must have more than one option, and participants in the meeting must take the time to consider the implications of adopting a recommendation and to understand its implications on other practices and programs. In 2021, for example, schools in the U.S. received billions of dollars in federal grant money to help them deal with the fallout of the global pandemic. If history is any guide, educational leaders were tempted, without lengthy discussion, to buy one program on top of another, leading inevitably to initiative fatigue. Every new curriculum program purchased, no matter how promising, vied for attention with the existing curriculum programs for the time and attention of teachers. Every new data analysis program, new assessment, and professional learning initiative competed for the one thing that even a billion-dollar grant cannot buy: the 25-hour day.

Although the Fearless Coach does not need to weigh in on client decisions on assessment, technology, and curriculum, it is absolutely essential that the coach ask the client, "What do you intend to stop doing in order to make time for this new program?" Our experience is that people are much better at addition than subtraction, and that explains the boxes of unopened materials, the streams of unused computer programs, and the short half-life of professional learning programs.

COACH PROVIDES IMMEDIATE CLEAR AND ACTIONABLE FEEDBACK

Some of the most effective team coaching we have observed occurs in the last two minutes of the meeting. For example, in schools and districts organized as professional learning communities (DuFour, et. al., 2006), collaborative teams of teachers join together to answer four questions:

- What do we want students to learn?
- How will we know if they have learned it?
- What will we do if they have not learned it?
- What will we do if they have already learned it?

At the end of collaborative team meetings, the coach can use the shorthand of learning, assessment, support, and enrichment to ask to what extent, if at all, these questions were addressed. While it is not necessary to address each of the four questions in every meeting, when a month of meetings goes by without addressing the need for support, then it's a sure sign that the team is more comfortable talking about lesson plans and unit design than about real student performance. Even high-performing teams benefit from immediate feedback, as the effort required to maintain great performance requires consistent support, encouragement, and feedback. The research is consistent that immediate feedback is vastly superior to delayed feedback if the objective is improved performance (Stenger, 2014). Therefore, a debriefing with the coach immediately after a meeting is superior to an elegantly written memo sent days afterward. In order to provide the most accurate and helpful feedback to the client, the coach should observe the client in their actual environment. Instructional coaches must, for example, be in the classroom when the instructor is teaching, rather than draw conclusions about teaching in the abstract—in the absence of students. Fearless Coaches should observe leaders in meetings, especially meetings that have an impact on the entire organization.

COACH LISTENS TO ALL OF THE PLAYERS, NOT JUST THE TEAM CAPTAIN

Eighteenth-century Scottish poet Robert Burns wrote words that should be deeply imprinted on the mind of every leader:

> O wad some Pow'r the giftie gie us
> To see oursels as ithers see us!
> (Burns, [1786] 2018)

Even the most perceptive leaders can have blind spots. They will insist, for example, that they welcome risk-taking and the errors that go along with it but seem stumped as to why their staff is not more innovative. The answer may lie not in a lack of ingenuity and creativity by the staff but in the common institutional fear that errors, no matter how innovative the intent, are punished and not rewarded. This creates the illusion of buy-in that is not the result of genuine support for the leader's ideas. Further, it can result in the silence of the staff—at least in the presence of the leader. Fearless Coaching requires fearless and consistent communication not only with the leader who is being coached but also with others in the organization. This need not be a formal 360-degree review, but it does require, at the very least, honest and confidential conversations that will allow the coach to test the assumptions of the client with direct evidence.

This requires a supreme degree of confidence and trust by the leader. When the leader receives unexpected feedback from the coach, the leader need not necessarily agree with it, but it is imperative that the leader respect the confidentiality of the process. I've witnessed the coaching relationship become undermined when the leader demanded to know who had provided feedback that the leader did not appreciate. My colleague, Dr. Mike Wasta, now an author and consultant and formerly the superintendent of schools in Bristol, Connecticut, used to say that while he knew that he needed to hear honest bad news, there were days when he felt that he had heard about all the honest bad news he could take. In fact, Wasta's great relationships with staff and community leaders allowed him to succeed in a very challenging environment. In his self-deprecating way, he would publish his "Oops Grams" to talk about mistakes and how he, and the entire system, could learn from them. This stands in remarkable contrast to leaders for whom any criticism or admission of error, any assessment or feedback that is less than outstanding, is a dagger in the heart and resisted at all costs.

Another reason the Fearless Coach must provide clear feedback and analysis of the entire organization, not just relying on conversations with the client, is that the idea of the single flawless leader must be challenged. The Leadership Performance Matrix (Reeves, 2008)[1] explicitly rewards leaders not for perfection, but for the personal and organizational resilience that results from candid admissions of error. This characteristic is at the very heart of what Harvard Business School professor Amy Edmonson (2018) describes as the fearless organization, and what my own research refers to as fearless schools (Reeves, 2021b). When it is safe to make mistakes, admit mistakes, and learn from mistakes, then greater learning, communication, and cooperation will follow.

COACH IS RELENTLESSLY GOAL-FOCUSED, LINKING ACTIONS TO RESULTS

Leaders are understandably focused on results. They and their governing boards want better student achievement, high attendance, improved discipline, more college credits, and a host of other results that stakeholders demand. But there is a problem with myopic focus on results, and that is explained by Campbell's Law. It states, "The more any quantitative social indicator is used for social decision-making, the more subject it will be to corruption pressures and the more apt it will be to distort and corrupt the social processes it is intended to monitor." Put simply: When a measure becomes a target, it ceases to be a good measure (Hess, 2018). The global pandemic provided particularly challenging examples of this. When the United States Department of Education required testing of students in reading and math in grades three through eight in the spring of 2021, after

---

[1] Free download at: https://static1.squarespace.com/static/56a6ae1c22482e2f99869834/t/6012d0317f0da2016a9e2c0e/1611845682131/Reeves+Leadership+Performance+Matrix.pdf

many students had missed half or more of a year of learning, it was no surprise that many parents simply refused to allow their students to take the test. There were widespread reports of cheating, especially when students were taking the tests from home. I know of not a single educator or leader who intends to allow the results of these tests to guide in educational strategy.

When in the fall of 2020, students were chronically absent and work was not turned in, some schools simply took those students off of their roster; so what had been a 50% attendance rate suddenly became a 90% attendance rate. Other school boards, in the face of pervasive student failure, insisted that teachers provide only pass/fail grades. Students who were not remotely close to proficiency in a subject passed the class. All of these distortions occurred because policymakers and leaders focused on results without understanding the causes behind those results.

Or consider a more troubling example. A school system, desiring to address the challenge of teenage obesity, measured the body-mass index (BMI) of scores of students. The problem is that there are a couple of ways to achieve the desired result of reducing BMI. The first is diet and exercise, accompanied by support and education. That seems like a lot of work. So let's take the second and easier path. You can also reduce BMI through drug abuse and eating disorders. Wouldn't you, as a parent or educator, want to know the causes and not just the results?

When the Every Student Succeeds Act (ESSA) was passed, it provided a great deal of flexibility to states and districts to reinvent accountability and to move from accountability systems that were solely based on scores to a more holistic approach (DuFour, et. al., 2017). The new ESSA repealed a great deal of the provisions of its predecessor statute, the No Child Left Behind Act (NCLB). Despite that flexibility, most states and districts produced accountability systems that can charitably be described as NCLB 2.0. Even if states refuse to consider an accountability system that focuses on causes as well as results, it is not beyond the ability of the leaders of districts and schools to carefully consider causes—that is, specific and measurable actions of educators and school leaders—to better understand how to achieve their goals. Fearless Coaches can be a key ally in supporting this analysis.

Consider this real example. Reading scores were down at almost every grade level, and the problem grew in intensity as students left the primary grades and entered the intermediate and middle-school grades. This was true before the pandemic, and it was especially true in the spring of 2021. The district had invested in the latest and best literacy programs and provided consistent and intensive training to their faculty and administrators. But what leaders failed to do was give the faculty the time necessary to address pervasive learning losses. Throughout the nation, as school leaders strive to return to something called normal, they are providing the same schedules and same time allocation for each subject as they had in 2019, before the pandemic. But in this case, the time allocated to reading declines in each successive year from third through sixth grade, and by seventh and eighth grade, students have had no explicit reading instruction. The evidence of students floundering in reading was clear, but leaders were willing to do everything except provide the time necessary to meet the crisis in literacy. While it is not the job of the Fearless Coach to make policy or implement it, it is clearly the responsibility of the coach to address the gap between the leader's intention and reality.

When all we have is effect data, then our attempts to explain the causes are limited to the data available. That is, we measure what is easy to measure rather than what is important. In the case of school data, the variables that are easy to measure include the students' eligibility for free and reduced-price lunch, their English Learning status, and their ethnicity. That is why these variables are often cited as the underlying causes of poor student performance, even when the important variables of teaching and leadership vary widely. It is the case, as the research of Karin Chenoweth (2017) and many others (Reeves, 2020a) demonstrates, that there are specific characteristics of schools serving low-income communities that also have high levels of achievement. These practices include effective classroom observation, frequent nonfiction writing, intensive intervention for students in need, and feedback to students and teachers that is accurate and timely. Therefore, when inquiring about the causes of achievement, the coach should never settle for vague allusions to poverty, language, and ethnicity, but should seek to understand the actual actions of leaders and classroom educators that are related to student results.

* * *

In this chapter we considered some key practices of the Fearless Coach. Although the coaches are not directly involved in the daily operations of the school or district, they can have a significant impact on performance. Because the coaches are not invested in past practices and decisions, they can provide a clear-eyed view of what is working and what is not. They can offer feedback to leaders and teams that is clear, actionable, and immediate. Coaches listen to a variety of stakeholders in order to help the leaders gain a better understanding of any gap between the leaders' perceptions and reality. And most importantly, the coach will help the leaders focus not only on results but on the underlying causes of those results. In the next chapter we will consider what clients should expect of coaches.

QUESTIONS FOR REFLECTION:

1. Based on your own experience as a coach or leader, what are some of the often-overlooked cause variables that you can consider in the future?
2. Think of a realistic situation in which the leader had to make a difficult decision. Based on what you have learned in this chapter, what are some ways of improving the decision-making process?
3. When you are coaching a leader, what questions would you like to ask of other people in the organization?

CHAPTER 4

WHAT THE CLIENT SHOULD EXPECT FROM THE COACH

> - ❖ Confidentiality: With Clear Exceptions
> - ❖ Candor: What Works and What Doesn't
> - ❖ Curiosity: Continual Search for the Causes of Barriers to Success
> - ❖ Confidence: Relentless Advocacy for the Client and the Organization
> - ❖ Clarity: Focusing on the Few Actions That Matter Most

TRUST IS THE ESSENCE OF FEARLESS COACHING, AND TRUST IS BUILT upon a solid foundation of mutually agreed upon expectations. In this chapter we explore what clients should expect from a coach. These understandings should be solidified before the coaching relationship begins. This chapter suggests the core elements of the coach-client relationship, including: confidentiality, candor, curiosity, confidence, and clarity.

CONFIDENTIALITY: WITH CLEAR EXCEPTIONS

Fearless Coaching is focused on improving individual and organizational performance. As a result, the client is not only the individual leader, but the client is also the school, the district, and ultimately the most important stakeholder in any educational system—the students we serve. Nevertheless, individual conversations between the coach and client must remain confidential. Within the confidence of the coach-client relationship, the client must feel free to express frustration, doubt, anger, stress, anxiety, and even career development outside of the client's present employer. These are discussions that almost never occur between the client and the client's supervisor or evaluator. These sensitive client-coach discussions will happen only if the clients know that these comments will go no further than their conversations with the coach. If the client is concerned about personal, physical, and psychological safety, the coach might waste a great deal of time and energy talking about educational strategy. While the coach is never to act as a psychotherapist, it is important that the coach knows of the emotional preoccupations of the client.

There are clear exceptions to the confidentiality rule, and that is when the coach perceives that failure to disclose information learned in a meeting with the client would expose students, the client, or other people to danger. Even if the client says, emphatically, "You can't tell anyone about this," then before the client says another word, the coach must remind the client that the veil of confidentiality is dropped when the coach perceives that a student, the client, or another person would be harmed as a result of the failure by the coach to disclose information.

For example, the client may want to discuss what the client describes as an especially delicate personnel matter because the client is considering terminating a teacher or not renewing the contract of a nontenured teacher. This is a familiar coaching conversation, as clients often need help toward rehearsing a difficult meeting. Perhaps the employee has been persistently ineffective during classroom observations, or the employee is often late or absent without notice. However, if the client explained that the reason for the termination was suspected child abuse by the employee and wondered if the employee should be permitted to resign in order to avoid a termination, the client has crossed the line, and the coach would have an obligation to inform the employer of this matter.

CANDOR: WHAT WORKS AND WHAT DOESN'T

Fearless Coaches are not engaged to be diplomats, rather to offer candid and clear observations. Though the coach should never be gratuitously negative in describing the client, the coach does not do the client or the students they both serve any favors by sugar-coating the obvious. If the coach knows, for example, that the superintendent's cabinet meetings have become a hotbed of political intrigue and gossip, and that the meetings are not achieving the goals the superintendent has established, then the coach has an obligation to say, "Dr. Richter, I'd like to offer my candid assessment of the last cabinet meeting I observed. Would that be okay?" If the client says to continue, then the coach might say something like this: "When I first was engaged to be your coach, you made it clear that the cabinet meetings were a source of frustration for you and others. You said that you wanted to shift the focus from reports and presentations to an emphasis on deliberation, inquiry, and decision making. I've looked at the agendas of the last four cabinet meetings and, as you know, I attended one of them as an observer. I need to let you know that I don't see much progress toward your goals. The meetings remain largely unfocused, with a few reports, some discussion, and a lot of grandstanding. There is no record of decisions made. You said that you wanted more deliberation, but I have not seen any evidence that you are being offered decision alternatives and that the entire group is helping to evaluate the advantages and disadvantages of those alternatives. I wouldn't be serving you and the district well if I failed to share these observations with you."

The ability of the coach to have such a candid conversation is predicated upon the idea that at their initial meeting the client and coach agreed on specific goals. The ultimate evaluation of the coach will not be the degree to which the client is comfortable but the degree to which the clients are sufficiently uncomfortable with the present state of affairs and therefore willing to change past practices in pursuit of their goals. I have seen some leaders who contend that they don't have the time for leadership coaching, but in these instances, one of the obligations of the coach is to examine how the leader's time is spent and to help develop a plan to save time. That might include not only reducing the quantity and length of meetings but also the familiar habits that devour the time of leaders, such as constantly checking email, texts, and other messages. These habits can steal hours that might be better devoted to important goals and, equally important, can deprive the leader of the focus and concentration needed to engage in the demanding cognitive work of an educational leader (Newport, 2021).

CURIOSITY: CONTINUAL SEARCH FOR THE CAUSES OF BARRIERS TO SUCCESS

Curiosity is an attribute that distinguishes the coach from the consultant. While consultants end their sentences with periods, and even exclamation points, the coach is more likely to end a sentence with a question mark. Examples of revealing questions might be the following:

- I can tell you are really frustrated by this challenge. Why do you think this challenge is so important for you?
- What are the barriers that stop you from taking the actions you would like to take?
- What have you already tried to do about this situation? Why do you think those actions have not succeeded?

- What do you think is the worst that would happen if you take the action you are contemplating? What is the worst that would happen if you fail to take the action you are contemplating?
- Who on your team do you trust to give you the most direct and unvarnished truth?
- What is the one thing that stands between you and achieving your goals?

It is tempting for a coach to attempt to answer these questions rather than allowing the client to do so. This is especially true if the coach has been in senior leadership positions and is fully capable of analyzing complex challenges and providing answers. They want to say, "Look, I'm the doctor, take two of these pills and call me in the morning if you don't feel better. Next patient!" But the coach is not the doctor; and when the coach seeks to streamline things by providing quick answers, the client will never build the capacity to operate independently. It is what Liz Wiseman (2010) called the difference between fixers and multipliers. Many school leaders are fixers. In fact, being a reliable fixer is why they were promoted. Have a problem? Janet can handle it. Whether it's a late bus, unruly student, upset parent, or finance form the district demands, we can always count on Janet to fix the problem. And so she does, from early in the morning to late at night, fixing every problem. Despite being exhausted, Janet revels in the role of fixer and the trust that people place in her.

But the problem is that when Janet is the perpetual fixer, no one else learns to address these problems. The entire organization becomes dependent upon Janet, and other people never learn to join Janet in solving these daily challenges. Besides, Janet might reason, "It takes too long to train somebody else, it's just faster to do it myself." In the short term, Janet is precisely correct. It does take time to train other people to handle complex challenges. But if Janet is ever to be liberated from her 24/7 electronic umbilical cord and get some much-needed rest, if she is ever to focus on complex intellectual challenges that leaders must encounter, then she will need to become a multiplier, helping others take responsibility. This will include, much to Janet's frustration, letting her colleagues not only take responsibility but also make some mistakes along the way. But if Janet does not tolerate mistakes, then her colleagues will quickly get the message that it's better not to try new things and will just let Janet remain the fixer. That strategy will not only burn Janet to a cinder, but it will deprive the school and district of potentially capable leaders who never had the opportunity to learn from Janet's expertise.

CONFIDENCE: RELENTLESS ADVOCACY FOR THE CLIENT AND THE ORGANIZATION

We are all biased, and the presumption that we can possibly be free of bias is preposterous (Collado, 2021). However, we can influence and even choose our biases. For example, teachers often have a positive bias about the ability of their students. When teachers engage in action research, they are indeed biased—and that is precisely the sort of bias that parents and students want to see. Leaders are biased in favor of the principle that individual performance can be improved, and that people are happier when they are achieving worthy goals and performing at a high level. Fearless Coaches should also be biased—biased in favor of the success of their clients and the educational systems they serve. This does not mean that they put blinders on when confronted with bad news, but it does mean that they are relentlessly confident and optimistic in the ability of their clients to rise to the challenge. This is particularly true when accountability systems are incomplete and potentially destructive, such as those systems that focus only on effects rather than causes. In these instances, the coach has an obligation to help understand the accountability data in a constructive manner.

Often, leaders and teachers in low-performing schools may complain about being held accountable for data that they cannot control. That's a reasonable concern, as neither teachers nor leaders can control variables like poverty, food security, access to technology, and home environment. But there is a difference between being responsible for data and, as coaches must stress, bearing responsibility for the leader's response to data. For example, if the data on today's weather report says that it's fifteen degrees Fahrenheit with blustery winds and snow, then none of those data points are the responsibility of the leader. However, the leaders and teachers in schools are absolutely responsible for their response to data. If they sent children out into the cold without warm coats, hats, mittens, and boots, then that is a failure of professional responsibility.

Similarly, leaders are not responsible for the fact that many students around the world lost significant amounts of learning time from March 2020 to June 2021. The leaders are not responsible for the fact that many ninth graders enter high school reading on an elementary-school level. But the leaders are absolutely responsible if they fail to respond to that data. When the coach sees leaders and their colleagues positively responding to data and carefully tracking their leading indicators—the underlying causes of student achievement—then the coach should be the advocate and cheerleader, helping the clients notice and reinforce every positive decision they are making.

CLARITY: FOCUSING ON THE FEW ACTIONS THAT MATTER MOST

Focus is one of the five core competencies of what I have called Equity and Excellence schools (Reeves, 2020a). Based on a review of more than 2,000 school plans, our research team learned that schools that focused on six or fewer priorities had significantly greater gains in student achievement than unfocused schools that had dozens of different priorities. The number *six* comes up in much of the literacy on effective leadership, as it is rarely possible for leaders to monitor more than about half a dozen indicators. That is why some schools and districts with the unfortunately named "war rooms" filled with charts, graphs, and statistics fail to send the essential messages to educators and leaders about which of the many indicators adorning the walls of the room are most important.

Similarly, coaches have a duty to help clients remain focused not only during coaching conversations but also as the leaders pursue their wider responsibilities. Fearless Coaches should, for example, be familiar with district strategic plans and school improvement plans before they start a coaching engagement. The coaches should look at minutes and agendas of staff meetings and cabinet meetings in order to gain an understanding of the leader's priorities. Most importantly, the coach should have the opportunity to see a week of the leader's calendar to notice the congruence, or lack of it, between the leader's values and goals and how the leader spends time.

For example, my work in one district revealed that principals were spending on average 2 ½ days every week out of their schools at district-mandated meetings, a requirement that is inconsistent with the district insistence that principals were to be instructional leaders, engaged in classroom observations and supporting instructional excellence. By contrast, I have seen districts show evidence of their respect for the time of their colleagues by drastically abbreviating meetings and making clear that if a participant's contribution was focused on one of ten agenda items, then that participant need only be present for that single agenda item and not the entire meeting. It's a cultural shift, but how people in an organization spend their time is an important reflection of the real goals and priorities of that organization.

* * *

In this chapter we considered the obligation of the coach to the client. These obligations include confidentiality, candor, curiosity, confidence, and clarity. It is imperative that these mutual expectations are clear to both coach and client before the engagement begins. In order for the coach to better understand the client's goals and needs, the coach should also invest time reading core documents such as strategic plans, school improvement plans, meeting agendas and minutes, and the calendar of the leader who is being coached. In the next chapter we will consider what coaches should expect from clients.

QUESTIONS FOR REFLECTION:

1. What are your experiences with providing candid feedback to a leader? When was it received well and when were your comments resisted?
2. What are some questions you might ask of a leader that reflect your genuine curiosity?
3. How can you help educational leaders focus on what matters most?

CHAPTER 5

WHAT THE COACH SHOULD EXPECT FROM THE CLIENT

- ❖ Availability: Making Coaching Sessions a Priority, without Interruption or Multitasking
- ❖ Openness: Allowing the Coach Access to Data, Teachers, and Students
- ❖ Interest: Genuine Curiosity about How to Improve Performance
- ❖ Vulnerability: Willingness to Discuss Organizational and Personal Challenges

EFFECTIVE COACHING RELATIONSHIPS ARE BASED ON TRUST. IN THE previous chapter, we considered what the client can expect from the coach. In this chapter, we describe the expectations that a coach should have of the client. This is a good opportunity to distinguish a client from a customer. While a customer seeks instant gratification, a client is focused on the long term. Customers can simply return the products they don't like for a refund. Clients, by contrast, should expect to be challenged and perhaps feel some discomfort. If the objective of the client is to change—the essence of improved individual and organizational performance—then we must have an honest conversation about the fact that change is difficult, uncomfortable, and even painful.

The reason that change is painful is that it represents a loss—a loss of previously held beliefs and attitudes, a loss of comfort and satisfaction with the way things are, and in the case of education, the loss of the personal and psychological identity that comes with expertise and mastery. When an educational leader has experienced a decade or more of perfect evaluations and a continuing stream of commendations and promotions, it's not easy to acknowledge that things could be even better, and that the path to improvement will involve personal and professional change. The wise coach will talk about these potential feelings of discomfort from the earliest days of a coaching relationship. While the coach need not be a nettlesome critic, it is vital for the coach to consistently compare where the client wants to be with where the client actually is. That is why the coach must reasonably not only expect that the client will make time for meaningful coaching in a distraction-free environment, but also expect that the client will become open to support and give the coach access to data, teachers, and students. The client should also match the coach in curiosity, genuinely seeking to learn how to improve. Finally, the client must be willing to be vulnerable and discuss openly and confidentially the organizational and personal challenges that they are facing.

AVAILABILITY: MAKING COACHING SESSIONS A PRIORITY, WITHOUT INTERRUPTION OR MULTITASKING

School leaders work exceptionally hard, with the average principal working in excess of 60 hours per week (Sparks, 2016). Administrators leading high-poverty schools have an even longer work week. For superintendents, the expectation in many systems is a nearly 24/7 job, with the expectation that leaders are present in schools during the day and at community events, board meetings, and school events in the evening and on weekends. Technology, which brought with it the promise of greater efficiency, has in fact been the source of long hours, with educational leaders expected to be on call at all hours of the day and night. Moreover, incessant interruptions from emails, texts, and calls lead to a fragmented day in which very little focused work can be accomplished. The work of leading teams, observing classrooms, and having deep conversations with teachers about curriculum and assessment cannot happen effectively when the leaders and their teams must deal with constant interruptions. That leaves only the early morning and evening hours for writing grant proposals, providing thoughtful feedback, and supporting teachers and students. That is why even the most efficient principal is, on average, working 60 hours—50% more than the typical 40-hour workweek—and the 60-hour number is just the average. That means that many leaders are working far more, and those serving the most challenging schools work significantly longer. While these leaders clearly can benefit from leadership coaching, a common response to this and other personal development opportunities is simply, "I'd like to, but I don't have the time." Even when coaching is required, when conversations between the client and coach are punctuated by interruptions, constant checking of electronic devices, and other distractions—there is little chance for the depth of communication on which effective relationships depend.

One way that effective coaches deal with this is to change the terminology. Rather than, "I'm busy," the client can say, "I have a commitment, so please don't interrupt me unless it is an emergency." Time with the coach is analogous to time with other important commitments—a consultation with the superintendent or board member, a date with a spouse, or watching a child's sporting event or concert. Few administrators would stop in the middle of a board meeting or child's concert to say, "Sorry for the interruption—I need to take this call." If the coaching relationship is to yield insight and value, then these conversations deserve the same level of commitment.

This commitment to availability requires the coach to be responsive to the needs of the client. The coach must ask, for example, "Please tell me the best time of day that you can give our work together your undistracted attention." If the client says, "My best times are six-thirty in the morning before the craziness starts," then the coach must accommodate the client's needs. Some clients simply don't have an hour for coaching, but they can engage in two focused 30-minute sessions. In such cases, the coach must accommodate the client.

OPENNESS: ALLOWING THE COACH ACCESS TO DATA, TEACHERS, AND STUDENTS

If the coach is to have a complete understanding of the successes and challenges of a leader, then the coach must have access to and will invest time in learning about the school and district. This means that the coach not only is immersed in publicly available data on key subjects such as achievement, attendance, and discipline, but also on other documents, such as strategic plans, school improvement plans, and other documents that reveal the aspirations of the leader. In addition, the coach should be able to have access to staff members and, where appropriate, observe classes so that the coach can compare the observations of the leader with the observations of the coach.

In addition to the formal data, such as state test scores, it is important for the coach to gain insight into other indicators that the leader believes are important, as well as indicators that the leader needs but does not have. We have noticed that leaders tend to have data that is easy to gather—scores, attendance, discipline, free and reduced lunch eligibility, and English learning status. What is missing are other key indicators. For example, when it comes to discipline, a key element of school culture, the nondiscretionary discipline issues including suspensions and expulsions are easy to document.

Nevertheless, it is equally important to get the story behind the numbers. This includes not only the major offences that lead to suspensions and expulsions but also the everyday office referrals. The coach should interrogate the data, seeking to learn the sort of violations that result in office referrals as well as the similarities and differences among teachers in making these office referrals. It is common that two different teachers with the same students have a significantly different frequency of referrals. The reason for these differences is rarely that the students change their behavior from one class to another; rather, it is the nature of the referrals. When we have analyzed office referrals, we have found not only that some teachers have dramatically higher referral rates than others, but that reported causes for referrals can sometimes be ambiguous and discretionary. The leading causes in many schools? Disrespect, student out of their chair, and failure to complete work. The higher the level of ambiguity and discretion, the greater the chance that the same offense leads to different consequences for different students.

The same analysis is revealing when the coach and leader consider student failures. The leading cause of failure is missing work. Yet some teachers manage either to get the work completed in class or to provide other methods for students to demonstrate proficiency, while other teachers continue to punish students for failing to complete homework. It is not the place of the coach to make policy about discipline and grading, but it is an essential part of the coaching conversation that the client and coach learn not just the superficial numbers in the data, but the underlying causes.

INTEREST: GENUINE CURIOSITY ABOUT HOW TO IMPROVE PERFORMANCE

Just as the coach must exhibit curiosity about the client and school environment, it is essential that the client shares that curiosity. The essential question is not how do the data support my hypotheses about teaching and learning. Rather, it is: I wonder what the data are telling us and what other information we need to gather to better understand this information.

A major stumbling block to individual and organizational learning is when the leader is positioned as the person with all the answers.

It is understandable why some leaders see themselves in this role. Many teachers appreciate the security of doing what the administrator wants, and others arrive on the job needing support to be as effective as they can be. Yet when the leader is ready with all the answers, there is the danger that the leader's answers are not quite as authoritative as they sound.

We all have our judgments colored by our experiences, and thus the leader might display an overreliance on their personal experience as a teacher, even if that experience is unrelated to the culture of today's classroom and the needs of today's students. Further, an effective coaching relationship requires a spirit of inquiry in which neither coach nor client provides glib answers, and both are willing to consider alternative perspectives and interpretations. Their mutual inquiry signals to the staff and students that this is a learning leader, not one who is magically invested with all the answers to life's most difficult questions.

One important way to understand the degree of curiosity of the client is to ask this question: What did you think was true about leadership five or ten years ago that today you know is not true? I have asked this question of thousands of leaders, and it is difficult to get a response. Perhaps there is a fear that admitting error would display weakness, and they believe that leaders can never show that they are weak and haunted by mistakes. I have tried to set the example by talking about things I thought were true in the past but have been proven no longer true according to current research, which indicates that I had been wrong. Some people will respond that this is a mark of integrity. They have learned to be wary of the speakers, writers, and researchers who are always conveniently right. Their data always conforms to their expectations, a sure sign of manipulation and outright fraud.

But there is another reaction when I talk about my mistakes. And it sounds something like this: If you were wrong and changed your mind about something you believed ten years ago, why should we believe you today? This question suggests that they prefer certitude over introspection. They are vulnerable to the speaker and writer who is often wrong but never in doubt. They are suckers for risible books such as *Leadership Secrets of Attila the Hun* (Roberts, 1990), which is preposterously inaccurate about both leadership and Attila. They cling to the theories propounded by personal journey stories of self-proclaimed leaders, not considering that it is unwise to generalize about all leadership responsibilities from a sample size of one. It is, after all, easier to read fables than to study the challenging discipline of leadership.

VULNERABILITY: WILLINGNESS TO DISCUSS ORGANIZATIONAL AND PERSONAL CHALLENGES

Perhaps the most difficult challenge for clients is being vulnerable, acknowledging what they need and what they don't know. This is why it is seldom successful when the person who is supervising and evaluating a leader also attempts to coach them. While coaching is a collaborative enterprise with both parties willing to share mistakes and vulnerabilities, conversations with evaluators are adversarial, with the client answering any evaluation that is less than perfect with a bevy of reasons that the evaluation is unfair. This devolves into a semantic game rather than a meaningful learning conversation.

Clients are most vulnerable when the coach is permitted to talk with other staff members and gain confidential feedback. The perceptive coach can distinguish between feedback from staff members that is intended to improve the school and provide effective communication, from feedback that reflects grudges and grievances from long ago.

* * *

In this chapter and the previous chapter we considered the mutual expectations of coaches and clients. We now proceed to Part II, in which we consider the foundations of why coaching is a vital source for individual and organizational improvement. Before you proceed, please review the Coaching Readiness Checklist (Appendix A). If you are the coach, it will help you determine, before the coaching engagement begins, the degree to which the client is ready for coaching. If you are the client or a person in a school or district who will be expecting other colleagues to receive coaching, this tool will be helpful in preparing you or your colleagues for an effective coaching relationship.

QUESTIONS FOR REFLECTION:

Vulnerability is a key expectation of the client, but how can you make a person feel comfortable and vulnerable with a complete stranger—the coach?

1. A key expectation of coaches is that they are genuinely curious. But clients must also be willing to learn with a spirit of curiosity. What are some questions you might ask of a client to better understand their degree of curiosity?
2. Ask prospective clients about the leadership books that have had the greatest influence on their role as leaders. How can you jointly reflect on these books, including those that are unburdened by research and relevance?

PART II
PASSION: THE ENERGY THAT DRIVES COACHING SUCCESS

In Part I, we explored the evidence that Fearless Coaching works. In Part II, we will consider how even the most busy and overwhelmed clients and coaches find the energy to persist through challenging times. During and after the global pandemic of 2020–2022, we have observed many leaders who were overwhelmed with fear, unwinnable arguments, and overwhelming demands on their time and energy. We know one superintendent who told us, "Every morning when I walk my dog, I get cussed out on one block for not keeping schools closed, and on the next block I get cussed out for not keeping schools open. Even though I'm pretty sure I'm not responsible for COVID, federal regulations, and state regulations, I'm the visible face of leadership that people can see and hate. It gets pretty tiresome." Nevertheless, leaders around the world persisted in their leadership responsibilities and, for many of them, leadership coaching was an essential part of their resilience, persistence, and survival. In the chapters ahead, we will consider the intellectual, emotional, and physical sources of energy that will sustain leaders and coaches in the post-pandemic world, a world of challenges, uncertainty, and the second-guessing by stakeholders that is the inevitable lot of leadership.

CHAPTER 6

CONTRASTING VISIONS OF THE FUTURE

> ❖ What Does the World Look Like When Coaching Is Successful?
>
> ❖ What Does the World Look Like Without Coaching?

EVERY COACHING RELATIONSHIP IS ULTIMATELY ABOUT CHANGE. In order to achieve the goals the client has established, there are typically three areas of essential change. First, the client must change: those changes might involve communication, personal organization, decision disciplines, and things as apparently mundane as the organization of the physical and virtual desk. Second, the colleagues—including peers, direct reports, and supervisors of the client—must change. It may seem unusual for the client to request a supervisor to change, but in almost every case we have observed, when the client wishes that a supervisor would change but no change ever happened, the most consistent reason is that the client simply did not ask the supervisor to change.

People and organizations are often the victims of inertia, assuming that present practices are just the way things are. But when proposed changes are supported by evidence or proposed as a pilot project, not a permanent change, individuals and organizations are often willing to acquiesce to the suggested change, even when the suggestion is made by someone who is not the most senior person. In addition to change by the client and the client's colleagues, the third type of change is organizational change. This includes changes in policies, procedures, expectations, meetings, accountability structures, and other key levers of performance.

WHAT DOES THE WORLD LOOK LIKE WHEN COACHING IS SUCCESSFUL?

Change efforts are almost always based on a vision. Sometimes the visions are crystal clear, such as, "Everyone learns, every day," or "100% of students are college and career ready," or "100% of students find a passion inside, or outside, of the classroom." These visions are so clear that everyone, from the 30-year veteran to the newest staff member, understands precisely what the vision means and how they might contribute to it. Other visions are gauzy, with vague multi-paragraph descriptions composed by a committee, in which every participant found it necessary to contribute a phrase. If a camel is a horse built by a committee, then incomprehensible vision statements are the result of the same committee when applied to wordcraft. If concision is so important, why is it so rare? The statement, "If I had more time, I would have made this letter shorter," has been misattributed to the usual cast of quotable characters—Mark Twain, Winston Churchill, and Ernest Hemingway, among many others. But the earliest known use of the expression was from French mathematician Blaise Pascal, who wrote in 1657, "I have made this longer than usual because I have not had time to make it shorter," (Pascal, 1658).

The coach and client should collaborate to establish a mutually acceptable vision for their work together, with the vision clearly expressing the future state the client wishes to achieve. The vision should be, well, visual—creating an emotionally compelling future state. For example, when I am coaching writers who seem to be stuck writing a book or dissertation, I encourage them to write the dedication page and a draft of the acknowledgments to their family, mentors, and friends who have inspired them on the journey and post that dedication and acknowledgments above their desk or wherever they write. Every time they are tempted—as almost all writers are—to procrastinate, they look at the family, mentors, and friends who are counting on them to finish the book and who have immense confidence that they can complete the task. Health and wellness coaches create visions of the future in which the client exhibits physical, psychological, and emotional health. Similarly, coaches can help clients craft a clear vision of the future if the coaching engagement is successful. This could, for example, be a literal vision of a student who is thanking the client for that student's excitement, engagement, and success. A one-minute video of real students could serve the purpose.

WHAT DOES THE WORLD LOOK LIKE WITHOUT COACHING?

While positive visions can be an important part of helping everyone in an organization, from the leader who is being coached to people throughout the organization, they are a necessary but insufficient impetus to change. The vision that is almost always overlooked in personal and organizational change efforts is the negative vision of the future without necessary change (Reeves, 2021a). This is a future in which, without the changes implemented by the client, students drop out of school and face a lifetime of poverty, unemployment, medical needs, and involvement in the criminal justice system. This is the future in which, without successful community engagement and the consequential support for school funding, there are 40 students in a classroom built for 30, students are sitting on the radiators and on the floor, and the teacher is despondent. This is the vision in which meeting participants are bored and disengaged because the leader did not successfully plan for the participants, agenda, and norms for the meeting.

Why is it so important to create a negative vision? Haven't we all been taught that students respond better to positive incentives than to punishment? That generalization is quite correct for students, but it is misleading for adults. Nobel Prize recipient and Princeton professor Daniel Kahneman (2013) and his colleagues have demonstrated repeatedly that adults fear loss much more than they enjoy gain. While there is no doubt that positive visions can inspire us, it is the negative visions that move us, especially when there are barriers—political, financial, and psychological—to making the difficult decisions that will lead to progress.

Personally, I find this research deeply troubling. My great preference is to be relentlessly positive. I'm the sort of person who, coming in from a rainstorm, will say to my soaked and uncomfortable neighbor, "Well, it's good for the farmer!" She replies, sullenly, that, "You must be one of those glass-half-full people." Indeed, I am, and my leadership career has been focused on creating positive visions of the future. But I ignore the research at my peril, as ignoring research will hurt me, my clients, and the organizations I serve. After all, I prefer to ignore the research that suggests that lasagna from Maria's in Boston's North End, followed by decadent pastries at Mike's, is not a meal that one might characterize as health food. Nevertheless, the pain of the cost of a new wardrobe with an expanded waist size keeps me from this indulgence, except for an annual splurge.

Similarly, I must say to clients on a regular basis that if I simply agree with everything they say without challenge, then I am failing in my role as coach. I must, for example, be able to say: "Dr. Solomon, you said that your top goal was to improve literacy for all of your students, especially those in the upper elementary and secondary grades. But Dr. Solomon, if you want to achieve that goal, you will need to allocate resources—teachers, intervention plans outside of the regular literacy block, and additional time—to achieve this goal. I know that this will risk enormous pushback from your staff, who are invested in the current schedule, and complaints from parents, who want their students to have more free time and electives—all of which will be affected by an increased emphasis on literacy. There may even be grievances by teachers and complaints at board meetings. But as your coach, I need to ask you to compare those sources of discomfort to the vision of middle- and high-school students who lack the literacy skills to succeed in school, who accumulate multiple failures in every subject, and who drop out and face a lifetime of challenges. There is no perfect option, Dr. Solomon, so you must choose which pain is better—the complaints of adults or the failures of students?"

I have been in leadership positions since I was 21 years old, and I do not like to be challenged like this, especially from some out-of-town leadership coach who is many years my junior. But experienced leaders have learned, sometimes through profound failures, that if they do not have someone courageous enough to challenge them, they will fail to consider decisions that are necessary but unpopular.

* * *

In this chapter we have made the case that coaches and clients must have two clear and compelling alternative visions of change. The first is the positive vision that reflects the satisfaction that accompanies the achievement of the client's goals. The second, more troubling, is the negative vision of what the world will look like without the change. While clients are understandably reluctant to create this negative vision, it is essential to move from doubt, inertia, and inaction to the decisive moves that effective change requires. Contemplating the necessity of negative visions may leave us feeling depleted and exhausted. In the next chapter we will consider the sources of emotional energy and how to restore our depleted souls and psyches.

QUESTIONS FOR REFLECTION:

1. Consider a change that is important to you, to a client, or to an organization you are serving. Create a positive vision of the future if that change is achieved. Feel free to use pictures, videos, or other images to make the vision lively and compelling.
2. Consider the same change and articulate the negative vision of the world if this change is not achieved.
3. Why do you think that people fear loss more than they value gain? How do you reconcile this psychological principle with the natural desire of coaches and clients to be positive?

CHAPTER 7
SOURCES OF EMOTIONAL ENERGY

> ❖ Purpose and Meaning
> ❖ Physical Health
> ❖ Relationships
> ❖ Service
> ❖ Mindfulness
> ❖ Connection with Children
> ❖ Self-Efficacy

WE LEFT THE PREVIOUS CHAPTER WITH A DREARY PICTURE OF THE client whose energy was depleted as a result of the need to confront the negative vision of the future if the client was unsuccessful in implementing change. In this chapter, we consider positive steps to promote the emotional energy of clients. Specifically, we will consider a variety of sources of energy, including emotional and physical energy.

PURPOSE AND MEANING

In great organizations, every stakeholder knows what they do and why they are there. For TED, the most powerful influence of innovation and information on the planet, their two-word mission is "Spread Ideas". For Google, it's "to organize the world's information and make it universally accessible and useful." For the Advent School, it's "Learn with passion. Act with courage. Change the world." For Nike, it's "to bring inspiration and innovation to every athlete in the world."

The stakeholders in these organizations, from the second grade student at the Advent School to the technology-support person at TED, to a shoe designer or assembler at Nike, know how they fit into the purpose and meaning of their organization. Coaches have an absolute obligation to understand the purpose and meaning that drives their clients. In some cases, this may be the organizational purpose, but in the vast majority of cases there is a personal passion that the coach must understand. Coaches must ask, "What makes you excited? What ignites your passion? What keeps you up at night?" In *The 7 Habits of Highly Effective People*, originally published in 1989 and one of the most influential books of the past three decades, Stephen Covey (2020) suggested that we write our own obituary. What would we want people to say about us at our funeral?

If it is too difficult to write one's own obituary, consider writing it for a friend or loved one. At my father's funeral, I did what I knew he would have wanted—not an oration about his heroism and quiet service, though his life embodied both of those qualities. Rather, I talked about his wife of more than 50 years who was in the pews to hear what I knew Dad would have wanted to say about her while she was still around to hear it. Don't wait for the funerals of those you love to tell them what they have meant to you. Say it now. And use that reflection as an opportunity to consider what you want said of you at or before your own funeral. That will unlock the key to the meaning and purpose that matters most. This is an ideal time for the coach to gently but clearly say to a client, "I know that you are deeply committed to your family, but you have established a set of goals that will require a twenty-five-hour day and eight-day week. You can't do that and maintain the commitment to your family that you know is most important. How can we work together to insure that, as you accomplish these important goals, you also have family time that is as sacred as any board meeting, labor hearing, or anything else that always takes priority on your calendar? How can we collaborate to build capacity so that the obligations do not always fall on you and deprive you of time with your family?"

PHYSICAL HEALTH

I know what it's like to complete seven marathons. I also know what it's like to be fifty pounds overweight. Hint: you can't eat like a marathoner if you don't train like one. The science of physical health is baffling, but the latest authoritative instructions, including from distinguished scientists, rotate through completely contradictory opinions every few years (Syed, 2021). Carbs are great! No, they are deadly. Avoid fat at all costs! No, eat all the bacon and hard cheese you want, just stay away from bread. White bread is awful, and whole wheat bread is healthy. As Matthew Syed has demonstrated, scientifically sound experiences have proven that *this* is true, *that* is the other way around—*and it doesn't make any difference.* Don't run after fifty! You can run until you die, and that includes with artificial knees and hips. Confused? It's too bad, because too many people have used the confusion to give up, resulting in a population in which more than a third of us are at risk for diabetes, cardiac disease, and a host of joint damage and pain that is associated with carrying around excessive weight.

This book will not pile on the specious advice about diet and exercise, as if there were anything like the average human to which such advice applies. Rather, the best advice that Syed offers is no prescription at all but a systemic inquiry about what works best for you. He notes, for example, that some people find sweet fruits like watermelon nearly toxic because of the way that they metabolize sugar, while others tolerate it well with no impact on their glycemic index. The same inconsistent effects are true of ice cream, steak, salads, and just about all foods. This is challenging, because it takes our physical health out of the hands of deeply fallible experts and places it where it belongs—in our own hands. Some very healthy people do not run marathons or, for that matter, do not run at all. They merely walk their dogs, slowly, not because they are logging miles, but because they enjoy the company of their pets and the wonders of the outdoors.

It is not the responsibility of the coach to take charge of the fitness and nutrition of the client. But the coach can, during in-person meetings, suggest a walking meeting. As the bard of the baseball diamond, Yogi Berra, supposedly said, "You can observe a lot just by looking." It's also very likely that lunch with a client will be slow, deliberate, and enjoyable, in contrast to the more common practice of a skipped lunch or fast food shoved down in minutes. Diets make hypocrites of us all, so it's very difficult for me to give advice about physical activity when I am sedentary and mindless about what I consume. Thus, the coach should consider carefully how to model, without words, the mental and physical resilience that we wish to achieve for our clients.

RELATIONSHIPS

Positive relationships are a key source of emotional energy and health. The strength of positive relationships is so strong that it affects not only health, but longevity (Yang, et. al., 2016). The irony is that, often, leaders attain their position as a result of positive relationships, but once they are in a leadership position, leaders can find themselves isolated. What relationships they have are likely to be transactional in that both parties are expecting something from the other. Leaders want followers to support their leadership vision and followers want the leader's approval and support. Whereas in strong interpersonal relationships, each party can be vulnerable, offering both support and acknowledging their need for support, transactional relationships are devoid of vulnerability. Both sides are hypervigilant, fearful of the consequences of failing to meet the expectations of the other.

In the context of Fearless Coaching, both coach and client must be aware of the tendency of a transactional relationship to take hold. After all, the client or the client's organization is paying for the time of the coach. What could be more transactional? This is precisely why the coach must invest time and emotional energy in getting to know the client, building trust, honoring confidences, and never judging vulnerabilities. Similarly, the coach cannot play the role of the all-knowing mentor, dispensing sage advice on every topic. Rather, the role of the coach is to ask questions—building the insight, self-awareness, and analytical capabilities of the client. In addition, the coach should understand the client's relationships inside and out of the workplace. The purpose of this inquiry is not to intrude into the client's personal life but to understand the sources of strength that the client brings to their daily responsibilities. The coach could ask, for example, "Who can you go to for advice or just to blow off steam, knowing that that person will never judge you?" Too often, leaders, and particularly the most senior leaders, are unable to answer that question. Perhaps they can share their burdens with a spouse or partner, but after a while, family members grow weary of the client bringing every workplace burden home.

Georgetown computer science professor and originator of the concept of deep work, Cal Newport (2021), recommends a daily ritual in which he instructs readers to review the actions of the day and the commitments of the next day and say, aloud, "Shutdown complete." Without such a consistent and audible ritual, Newport argues, we never shut down, and we tend to bring all of the troubles of work home. This is exemplified by the leader who never unplugs and, often proudly, answers emails and texts during family dinners and in bed.

The difficulty in finding genuinely nonjudgmental relationships may explain the increasing demand for psychotherapy, the clinician with whom clients can confess their deepest fears and vulnerabilities. While the global pandemic of 2020–2022 is associated with a dramatic increase in the demand for psychotherapy (Caron, 2021), increasing levels of stress, anxiety, and substance abuse were present well before the onset of the pandemic. While therapy is certainly appropriate for anyone dealing with mental illness, even the best therapist does not replace the human need for a positive relationship.

SERVICE

There is a deep-seated human need for a life of meaning and purpose. Even in the depth of despair and deprivation in the Nazi concentration camps, Viktor Frankl (1946) was able to find hope and meaning in life and was able to encourage others to find purpose in even the simplest acts of kindness and support for others. The essence of service is that there is no expectation—ideally no possibility—of reciprocity. The act of service itself, not the actions of the person being served, is what gives service its meaning. In many religious traditions, support for the widow and orphan, and by analogy, the helpless of the world, is a solemn duty. Many people find great joy and peace in providing anonymous help to those in need. Coaches might therefore inquire about the sources of joy, meaning, and purpose for the client outside of work. In education, the immediate default is that we help children, as well as the educators and administrators whose life work is teaching and helping students, become successful adults.

Unfortunately, many evaluation instruments for leaders and teachers create incentives for precisely the opposite of service. When competitive rewards are given only to those with the highest test scores, then the resulting institutional incentives are not for collaboration and mutual support. Rather, such incentives avoid supporting—and at worst, undermine—teachers in other schools and by extension, their students. In an international study of financial incentives for teachers, Michigan State professor Scott Imberman (2015) concludes: "There is no evidence that incentives tied to specific exams result in improvements in other measures of academic performance, suggesting a lack of general improvements in knowledge."

Indeed, some financial incentives had counterproductive effects leading to lower achievement. The evidence has not stopped state legislators in the United States from the conviction that if only teachers were offered an extra $500, then at last the teachers would reveal their hitherto secret teaching strategies that would lead to improved student learning. Although I will argue for more financial and professional recognition for teachers, the idea that anyone was enticed into a career as a classroom teacher for its financial rewards is, on its face, ridiculous. Indeed, studies of teachers leaving the profession, even in the positions that sometimes receive bonuses, such as science and math, the primary reason for abandoning their career is almost never financial—but poor working conditions (Reeves, 2018). Worse, there is evidence that financial rewards actually undermine performance, especially when the rewards are associated merely with doing one's job well (Ledford, et. al., 2013).

Imagine a physician being rewarded only for producing positive outcomes for patients. By the logic of extrinsic rewards, this should lead to better health for all of us. But the opposite is true. If physicians are only rewarded for positive outcomes, then their incentive is to avoid the most difficult patients and not even attempt surgery on those with the gravest conditions. Better to let them die than have a negative outcome on the physician's scorecard (Edmondson, 2018).

MINDFULNESS

A substantial literature has grown around the practice of mindfulness and the positive psychological and physical results of the consistent practice of mindfulness (Salzberg, 2020). While many people find a regular practice of mindful meditation to be useful, the principle of mindfulness has broad applicability. When we are mindful about eating, then we can savor the food rather than gobbling it down as nothing more than a source of fuel. When we are mindful about relationships, we give our undivided attention to those we care about. One needn't practice meditation to notice the difference in a coaching meeting when both client and coach are fully engaged, compared to a conversation in which the parties are giving the process only superficial attention while they check emails and texts, ever vigilant that something more important than the present conversation may arise.

Coaches can help clients in two very specific ways: self-awareness and resilience. Both of these qualities are enhanced through deliberate mindfulness (Eva, 2017). Self-awareness is a skill to be developed, and it takes some practice. Early in the coaching relationship, clients should take the Brief Strengths Test or, if time permits, the longer (240-question) VIA Survey of Character Strength, both of which are available for free at the University of Pennsylvania website: https://www.authentichappiness.sas.upenn.edu/. The role of the coach is to ask for examples of when clients have applied their top strengths and how the clients felt when those strengths were used. Critically, the coach and client must explore why those strengths are not used more frequently in the daily life of the client and what the barriers are to relying to a greater extent on those strengths.

CONNECTION WITH CHILDREN

Our care for children is the reason we entered the field of education in the first place, and both educators and leaders, from the classroom to the boardroom, have the opportunity to influence generations of students. The challenge for the busy leader is engaging with children on anything more than a ceremonial basis. The late Dr. Stan Scheer made a point of putting himself on the substitute teacher list 20 times each year. Most of the students had no idea who Dr. Scheer was, and in the capacity of substitute teacher, the superintendent learned first-hand the joys and challenges of classroom teachers. He once told me that working in a kindergarten class was one of the most physically demanding tasks that this military veteran had ever done. This duty required, he recalled, about 100 deep knee bends every hour along with the ability to go hours at a time without a bathroom break. The physical challenges aside, he was able to share the joy of discovery with students as they achieved breakthroughs in learning, whether sounding out words in the primary grades or thinking about literature and history in new ways for older students.

The connection with children is important for coaches as well as clients. When coaching meetings take place at the client's location, it is useful to make time to wander the halls of a school and drop in on a few classrooms. These activities give the coach an authentic view about what the client sees as important or unimportant. Little gestures count. For example, we have accompanied clients through hallways that are spotless, except for the piece of paper or soft drink can that's on the floor. Some clients stop and pick up the trash, expressing with their actions that everyone, including students, teachers, and leaders, takes pride in the appearance of their hallways. By contrast, we have been with leaders who live in chaotic environments of unfiled papers around their offices and the offices of counselors and other administrators who are similarly disorganized and trash in the hallways and playgrounds. In these schools, classrooms show similar signs that the adults simply don't care about their environment. Books are strewn around the floor, closets are disorganized, and the teacher's desk is covered in a pile of papers. This, too, sends a message about how these leaders tolerate disorganization. Whatever the leader tolerates can be regarded by everyone else in the system as encouragement.

These observations, both favorable and unfavorable, are only possible when leaders get out of their offices and make connections with students. Some principals make a point of being outside the entrance of the school on even the coldest days and greeting every student by name. Others retreat to the relative comfort and security of their office, noticing students only when they are in trouble. The worst reason in the world to become a school administrator is an aversion to students. Nevertheless, we see too many teachers secure their administrator license not to make a positive difference for students but to gain greater distance from them.

SELF-EFFICACY

The importance of efficacy is overwhelming (Moore & Margaret, 2020; Cook, et. al., 2020; MacKie, 2016). In John Hattie's landmark synthesis of meta-analyses, he found that the impact of collective efficacy was more than twice as great as prior knowledge (Donahoo, et. al., 2018). This combination of the way educators think, feel, motivate, and behave is so powerful that every coach must be attentive to the degree to which clients reflect efficacy in their coaching conversations. It is essential that coaches compare the words of the clients with their actions. It would be difficult to find a leader who does not claim to believe in the power of efficacy. Nevertheless, the coach must listen carefully for contradictory messages. It is difficult to reconcile the claim of efficacy with the frequent allegations that "Our demographics just don't allow us to ____" and "When the parents don't value education, there isn't much we can do."

Earlier in this book, we have recommended an exercise to address the depth of efficacy in any group of educators and leaders. It bears repeating here. To really get at the root of efficacy, we recommend the following exercise, done either with the client or with their entire staff. Simply ask, "What are the causes of student achievement?" Ask the participants to put each cause on a separate piece of paper. These causes might include factors such as poverty, access to drugs, teacher engagement, student-teacher relationships, food insecurity, attendance, and dozens of other factors.

To assess the degree of efficacy, the coach should then divide these pieces of paper into three piles. In the first pile are factors which the client can neither control nor influence. These include things that happen, or fail to happen, at home well beyond the reach of the school. The second pile includes the factors that the leader cannot control but can certainly influence. This includes factors such as transportation, the provision of nutritious meals for students, and attending to the psychological well-being of the student. The third pile includes the factors that leaders and teachers can both influence and control. This includes factors such as effective feedback in the classroom, the maintenance of a safe and secure environment, a relentless focus on academic achievement, and the provision of relevant and engaging lessons for students.

Now that there are three piles—factors we can neither control nor influence, factors we can influence but not control, and factors we can both influence and control—the question is how many factors are in each pile? When the second and third piles are greater than the first pile, then the faculty and leadership of that school or system can claim to be efficacious. That does not diminish the serious impact of factors in the first pile. Poverty, homelessness, food insecurity, and drugs, just to name a few factors, are serious. But to the extent that they are not under our control, it is not a great expenditure of leadership and faculty time to perseverate about them. Rather, the faculty and leaders with high levels of efficacy focus on the factors that they can influence and control.

***

In this chapter we considered sources of emotional energy and how the Fearless Coach can promote the emotional health of clients. We considered the essential nature of finding purpose and meaning—the emotional sustenance on which the ability of clients to overcome challenges depends. In addition, we applied the research on physical health, relationships, mindfulness, and self-efficacy in order to maintain and increase the emotional energy of our clients. In the next chapter we consider the sources of emotional drag that afflict nearly every client in every organization, no matter how well-intentioned the leaders may be.

QUESTIONS FOR REFLECTION:

1. What do you believe your greatest strengths to be? How are your beliefs about your strengths similar to or different from the results of the VIA Assessment of Character Strengths?
2. What are the barriers to you making greater use of your strengths?
3. Describe how a Fearless Coach might help clients make better use of their strengths.

CHAPTER 8

SOURCES OF EMOTIONAL DRAG

- ❖ Self-Criticism
- ❖ Fragmentation
- ❖ Distance from Children
- ❖ Learned Helplessness
- ❖ Loss of Integrity
- ❖ Substance Abuse and Addictive Behaviors

ORGANIZATIONAL DRAG IS A WELL-DOCUMENTED PHENOMENON (Mankins & Garton, 2017) in which the impact of ineffective deployment of time, talent, and energy sap an organization of its ability to accomplish its mission. In this chapter we consider the cousin of organizational drag: emotional drag. Just as organizational drag saps the energy of teams and organizations from the top, emotional drag saps the energy of the people who comprise the organization. As we consider each factor that leads to emotional drag, it is important to avoid blaming the victim. By analyzing the factors that affect the individual, we are mindful of the potential complaint that, "If only . . ." team members were more responsible and better behaved, then all would be well with the organization. That is somewhat like blaming the malfeasance of the liver for the behavior of the alcoholic. The thesis of this chapter is one of shared responsibility throughout the organization, as we all share the same pathologies. The good news is that we can also share the same solutions in pursuit of individual and organizational health.

SELF-CRITICISM

Highly effective leaders not only expect the best of their colleagues, but they set similarly high standards for themselves. This is an admirable trait until the demands that leaders place on their shoulders become overwhelming and result in relentless self-criticism. Rather than inspiring everyone in the organization to support its mission and values, the oppressive voice of the inner critic suggests that the leaders are never satisfied, and if they cannot satisfy themselves with their hard work, great education, long experience, and other wonderful qualities, then what chance do others in the organization have to meet the irrational expectations of the leader?

There are constructive steps that leaders can take to avoid this destructive self-criticism. To be clear, this is not about the leaders simply feeling good about themselves, as the fictional Stuart Smalley did on *Saturday Night Live*. Smalley's refrain was "I'm good enough, I'm smart enough, and gosh darn it, people like me." This parody of self-help publications was funny because it was so authentic, with demonstrably incompetent people feeling good about themselves.

There are ways for clients to engage in appropriate introspection and self-awareness without entering the territory of destructive self-criticism. Executive coach Melody Wilding suggests labeling the inner critic with a preposterous name, such as Darth Vader. Her client kept a plastic toy of the evil genius of *Star Wars* just to cut him down to size and recall that he had no power at all (Wilding, 2021). In addition, Wilding suggests avoiding generalizations, in which a single failure or embarrassing error leads to an exaggerated sense of doom, with the inner critic shouting, "You always mess this up and you never prepare adequately." Further, irrational self-doubt can be attenuated by asking what-if questions such as: What if the board loves my idea? And what if this idea revolutionizes the way that we achieve our goals?

This is not irrational positivity; rather, it is a nuanced approach that balances the opposing forces of critical and optimistic viewpoints.

Wilding also suggests allocating specific times for critical self-review. At Creative Leadership Solutions, we have long had the "five-minute rule" in which our colleagues are permitted to strut around like a peacock for 4 minutes and 59 seconds when they do something exceedingly well or win an important prize or achieve other recognition. But after those five minutes, they must get back to work. Conversely, when we mess up, we are permitted to feel awful about it for 4 minutes and 59 seconds, and then get back to work. It's a good discipline for any team, and it allows the team leader to say to the person who is indulging in relentless self-criticism, "Sorry—five minutes have elapsed, and self-loathing is now officially over."

Finally, Wilding suggests that we expand our definition of success. The fact that an idea is not adopted by a governing body or senior leadership team does not mean that the person proposing it is incompetent. In fact, the provision of different ideas strengthens decision-making and avoids the "take it or leave it" decision patterns that often confront senior leaders. The evidence for mutually exclusive decision options is clear (Lafley & Martin, 2013; Reeves, 2021a). In the best decision-making cultures, leaders require options, and the people presenting the option that is not selected are as valuable to the decision-making process as those who present the decision options that are selected.

FRAGMENTATION

People do not get into education in order to hurt the children whom we serve. But in most coaching conversations we have observed, the daily and hourly priorities are far afield from our most noble objectives. Fragmentation is not an accusation, but a reality (Reeves, 2013; Newport, 2016). Who can blame an educator or school administrator for being fragmented when, in the course of a normal day (or more precisely, an hour) they are inundated with texts, voice mails, and emails. Their fragmentation is not a sign of weakness but of their dedication: I have to get back to these parents, or they might complain to the administration! I must reply to my principal, or she might write me up for being nonresponsive! I know that I have an essential small group of students right now, but there is a lawyer who is threating to sue the district, my principal, and me if I don't respond promptly! Fragmentation, in brief, is not the pathology of the individual teacher or administrator, but of the system. Note to the spouses and partners of educators and school administrators: If your loved one comes home cranky, it's not about you but a condition that, in the world of education, we call "normal".

DISTANCE FROM CHILDREN

Every reader of this book entered our profession because we love children. Yet the fundamental cause of fragmentation, frustration, and futility is rooted in the distance between the classroom educator and administrator and the children we love. We knew their names, their interests, their hopes and their fears. And then—we displaced those personal relationships that gave children joy and gave ourselves purpose and meaning, with bureaucracy. We supplanted people with paper. This is no knock on the administrators demanding the documentation, as they, too, were once teachers who entered our profession because they loved kids but, as the demands of their jobs increased, have not been face-to-face with a child for a very long time.

LEARNED HELPLESSNESS

The origins of pathological behavior are rarely ingrained; rather, they are learned. Learned helplessness (Rodin, 2014) is not the result of malice; it is the result of years of futile efforts of educators and leaders who attempted, without success, to support students. Despite our best efforts, we fail, and fail again. The antidote is learned optimism

(Seligman, 2007), in which both children and adults become accustomed to a result that is associated with their earnest efforts.

The skillful coach could present a scenario of the struggling student or colleague and ask the client to make a prediction about the future. In these essential coaching conversations, there are two paths. The first path is one of learned helplessness: "There is nothing I can do—the politics, union, parents, kids, culture—it's all just impossible." The fundamental job of the coach is to interrogate these presumptions and ask, gently but persistently, "What evidence do you have that leads you to this conclusion?" The coach can, with deep empathy, acknowledge that there are toxic politics, irresponsible parents, disruptive students, and a toxic culture. All of this may be true, the coach can acknowledge. But with gentle persistence, the coach can also inquire, "Even with these conditions, is it possible that you can make a difference in order for these students to be successful?"

There are three possible responses to this essential coaching question. The first is, "Yes, despite all of these obstacles, I can still make a difference." This response leads to the coaching conversation that focuses on solutions. The second response is, "I'm not sure," and this is the fertile territory in which coaching can make the most profound difference. The coach and client can collaborate to inquire in detail about where the coach can make the greatest difference and gather systematically the evidence about the impact of the client on student results. The third potential response of the client is, "No—nothing I do makes a difference. I'm just a helpless pawn in the chess game of life."

Putting aside for the moment that in the game of chess, pawns can win victories over kings, the coach is not called upon for intellectual gymnastics. Rather, this is the time to ask with compassionate directness, "If you really believe that you make no difference in the lives of children, can I help you find a different career path?" This is neither challenging nor accusatory, but compassionate. Some people—indeed, most people—are not destined to be educators and school leaders. When the coach encounters these people, the kindest and most compassionate approach is neither to salve their wounds nor to reassure them that things will be better, and that it's really bad but not their fault. The kindest and most compassionate approach is to say with clarity and compassion, "It looks as if this is just not the right fit for you, and I'd like to help you communicate that to your supervisor and to help you find a fit, either inside or outside of education, that will give you the joy and satisfaction you deserve." Exiting our profession need not involve blame or derision. It's just a different choice. Most educators I know would not want to be auditors for the Internal Revenue Service. That doesn't mean they are bad people—it's just not the right fit for them. When a coach encounters someone who is not the right fit for education, it is not an accusation. It's just an observation that they might find joy and purpose elsewhere.

LOSS OF INTEGRITY

Educators are, in their heart of hearts, people of great integrity. They are profoundly honest and sincere. They bear the literal meaning of *integrity*—integrating their behavior with their values—on their sleeves. In every conversation with students, colleagues, and supervisors, they speak and act with integrity. Because their words match their actions, they never temporize. Rather, they insist, "I know that James doesn't meet the criteria for the gifted and talented program, but I've seen his work, and despite his scores and occasional behavioral issues, he deserves to be in the class with our highest performing students." They will challenge discriminatory policies and go to the mat for students. "Yes, this is the third time that Shadee was sent to the office, but to suspend her will be devastating, and I will stake my job on getting her back into class."

It's clear what integrity is: the integration of our values with our actions. But it is perhaps less clear about what a compromise in integrity looks like. For the most part, it is silence. The lack of integrity is rarely something brazen, such as cheating and altering student test scores. Rather, the sort of integrity compromises that this chapter considers are the silence of good people who remain indifferent in the face of cheating, discrimination, evident bias, and clear harm to students based on gender, race, economic status, or other factors. This is the teacher or school administrator who sees the bright and capable third-grader held back because of a failure-to-meet-the-cut score on a state-mandated reading test, knowing that retention dramatically escalates the probability that this capable student will drop out of school and suffer a lifetime of unemployment and poverty. This is the well-intentioned teacher and administrator who stand by while a high-school student is expelled for well-justified anger against the racism of other students and staff members. It is the anger that is punished, not the racism of staff and students. "I know it's wrong," these people say, "but it's policy—that's just City Hall, State Legislature, Congress, or who knows what. There's just nothing I can do about it."

These bystanders are not evil. They are not necessarily racists. They are just like most people who, confronting uncomfortable situations, prefer to walk on by rather than intervene. We judge them at our peril because we must recall the times when we could have intervened but failed to do so. But despite this litany of excuses, the lack of integrity is not merely about overt cheating but about the countless instances in which our actions failed to match our words. I've intervened in precisely two fights in my long career as a leader, but to my great shame, I know of dozens more in which I should have entered the fray. I share this only to show that this chapter is not about hectoring others, but holding all of us, including myself, accountable for what integrity really means.

SUBSTANCE ABUSE AND ADDICTIVE BEHAVIORS

It takes an exceptionally perceptive and skillful coach to discern normal-if-obnoxious behaviors from the dysfunctional behaviors associated with substance abuse. In casual parlance, there are many behaviors that might be labeled as nothing more than difficult, obnoxious, blaming, insulting, or the common behavior of people who are just plain insensitive and nonempathetic jerks. To be clear, coaches are not called upon to be addiction counselors or therapists. Nevertheless, they serve important roles in helping clients seek the treatment and support that they need when the source of their maladaptive behaviors is in school. Appropriate questions might include:

- "You seem really upset. I need to ask, have you been drinking?"
- "I can tell you that you are not very focused on our conversation. Can you tell me what that's all about? It's fine if you want to talk later, but it would help me to know if you're stoned right now."
- "You have said the same thing three times in the last few minutes, so I need to ask you if you are feeling okay. If you'd like to take a break, that's fine."

It's not the responsibility of the coach to deal with substance abuse, but it is absolutely the responsibility of the coach to have accurate feedback from the client. If the client cannot provide accurate feedback, then the most helpful feedback that the coach can provide to the client is, "We did not have a productive meeting in our last session, and I hope that we can get back on track next meeting." This is neither accusatory nor diagnostic but simply a statement of the truth: Clients who are under the influence cannot provide effective engagement with the coach.

* * *

In this chapter we have explored how the attitudes and actions of clients can undermine their success. While the coach is neither a therapist nor an addiction counselor, the coach can and must notice and inquire about behaviors and thinking patterns that undermine the client. The coach can inquire directly about the evidence to support negative client perceptions about their own performance and future as well as their negative attitudes toward children. Note that a coaching session is not a debate in which the coach emerges victorious as a result of superior evidence. Rather, effective coaching conversations are focused on questions that challenge the client's maladaptive beliefs and behaviors and reinforce the client's strengths. In the next chapter we turn our attention to the critical issue of focus.

QUESTIONS FOR REFLECTION:

1. Think of a time when you engaged in destructive self-criticism. How did you emerge from this very dark psychological space? How did a colleague, friend, or coach help you?
2. How many to-do lists do you have right now? How many total items are on those lists? What is the probability of you completing 100% of these tasks? How can you move from fragmentation to focus?
3. How can you reignite your passion for children? How can you build relationships and restore the joy of shaping young lives?
4. How have you dealt with substance abuse in a family member or colleague? What worked and what didn't? What was the impact—personal and organizational—of untreated addiction?

CHAPTER 9

THE POWER OF FOCUS

> ❖ Focus and Student Results
> ❖ Focus on Personal Satisfaction and Happiness
> ❖ Focus and Organizational Health
> ❖ The Power of the Garden Party and the Not-to-Do List

ONE OF THE REASONS WE LOVE EDUCATORS AND SCHOOL LEADERS IS their indomitable spirit. They routinely take on challenges that seem overwhelming, ranging from traumatized students and staff members to stultifying bureaucracies that sometimes are more interested in process than results. Their to-do lists are endless and their energy is boundless, at least until they crash, utterly spent and exhausted. That was true before the global pandemic led teachers to manage classes through means that ranged from sophisticated technology to telephones, to mailed-in packets of work, to sidewalk visits to let students and families know how much they missed them and needed them to be engaged in school.

It is not uncommon to hear many teachers and administrators referred to as heroes. But as much as I deeply admire these professionals, I must point out this essential law of the universe: Heroism is not a sustainable strategy. However glorious their battles and soaring their rhetoric, most heroes that we celebrate from ancient Greece and Rome had one thing in common: They died in battle. The goal of this chapter is not to surrender to overwhelming pressures but to help coaches, teachers, and leaders focus on the few priorities that will best serve students and at the same time allow the professionals to enjoy the satisfaction of jobs well-done, rather than persevere in a perpetual state of exhaustion and frustration.

FOCUS AND STUDENT RESULTS

In a test-driven world, it is common for leaders, policymakers, and especially critics of public education to focus on results as measured in test scores. Every great teacher and leader I know is unafraid of accountability, but we do wish that accountability not only considered test scores but also reflected the many other things that educators do every day that lead to results. The Every Student Succeeds Act (ESSA) granted states broad discretion to consider additional variables in designing their accountability systems (DuFour, et. al., 2017). Despite the opportunity to create more holistic accountability systems that could include growth in achievement during the school year—and, critically, the actions of teachers and leaders that lead to student results—educational accountability in the United States remains dominated by the results of annual tests.

Fearless Coaches and the teachers and leaders served by these coaches must not settle for annual tests as their only indicators of success. Harvard Business School professors Teresa Amabile and Steven Kramer (2011) have conducted research that demonstrates convincingly that we are most motivated not merely by annual goals but also by the ability to see objective growth and improvement every day. When I have asked teachers and leaders to tell me the hallmarks of the most effective feedback they have ever received, they invariably express the desire that feedback is timely. For teachers, feedback should be provided in a face-to-face conversation (never an email or text) on the same day as the observation. When coaching a school administrator's facilitation of a staff meeting, the coach has a responsibility to provide immediate feedback—again, on the same day that the observation took place. Only in this way can the coach link causes—the actions of teachers and leaders—to student results.

The coach can also help educators track results in creative and encouraging ways that do not depend upon printouts of graphs of test scores alone. For example, we have seen a wonderful first-grade class in Virginia in which each student maintained a chart of their own progress toward learning goals so that they could end every week with the confidence that they were moving closer to their goals. A creative middle school faculty in Ohio had a school-wide emphasis on nonfiction writing, one of the strategies with the greatest impact on all other areas of student performance (Reeves, 2020a). Rather than post scores on writing tests, the teachers created displays that showed the written work of individual students as the year progressed. The growth in complexity and coherence of the writing was impressive, as if the work displayed for November could not have been the same student whose September essay was displayed next to it.

Coaches can use examples such as this to make it clear that "results" need not be restricted to standardized test scores but can be displayed in ways that show the progress of students during the year. This is especially important because, as we considered in the previous chapter, there are many factors that can adversely affect student performances that teachers can neither influence nor control. However, the display of same-student-to-same-student work is a compelling illustration of the power of the classroom educator to make a difference. It was, after all, the same student, with the same home environment, same attendance, same everything. The only difference between the September work that was barely decipherable and the thoughtful and well-reasoned essay in November was the work of the classroom educator and the willingness of the building administrator to create the time and space for writing in every classroom.

FOCUS ON PERSONAL SATISFACTION AND HAPPINESS

The helping professions—educators, social workers, nurses, and many others—are often typified by the sacrifices that professionals make. These sacrifices include time away from family, high levels of stress and anxiety sometimes imperiling their own health, and a lack of economic security. So why do they do it? The most common answer that we hear is that educators at every level have a bone-deep belief that they are making a difference. Richard Ingersoll of the University of Pennsylvania has studied why people remain in education and, of equal importance, why they leave. Contrary to popular conception, it is not a lack of money that drives people out of the profession that they once loved; rather, it is working conditions that are disrespectful and unsafe (Reeves, 2018).

Although many schools are starting to take self-care for teachers and administrators seriously, they may not notice the irony of requiring staff members to report to a mandatory workshop on stress and anxiety reduction, a requirement that can easily induce more stress and anxiety as the workshop participants know that they are losing vital time with students. I do not wish to diminish the very real impact of stress and anxiety on the health and performance of staff members (Cook, et. al., 2020; Kang, et. al., 2014). Coaches have a clear role to play and should include as part of every coaching conversation this simple question: "What are you doing to take care of yourself?" The answer too often is a plan to take a vacation the following summer or the statement, "I just don't have the time." While Fearless Coaches are not in the business of providing medical advice, they can nevertheless pose the question and let the silence hang in the air for a moment. Coaches not only care for clients on a personal level but also know that there is an obligation to the school, the district, and the students whom we serve to have teachers and leaders who are as healthy and happy as possible. Anxiety is a communicable disease, and the best evidence of that occurs every year during state tests. Students pick up on the fears of the adults who, if the scores are not good, may face transfer or unemployment. Fear is never a good strategy to motivate performance in students or adults (Reeves, 2023). When schools have a climate of fear, neither students nor adults will take any risks or admit error publicly; these conditions undermine learning.

While we cannot expunge the fear that pervades many educational settings, coaches can ask questions that help clients focus more on hope than despair. For example, every coaching conversation should include the question: "What are a couple of things for which you are grateful today?" Gratitude, if only expressed in a journal, has a significantly positive impact on our dispositions (Marshall, 2019). Leaders who take a few minutes to write a personal note to a teacher or other staff member at the end of every day not only encourage the colleague who is surprised by this genuine act of appreciation but also find their own frame of mind more positive. When despair is displaced by optimism, the results are positive in both psychological and physical terms (Conversano, et. al., 2010). In addition to acts of appreciation, physical movement is strongly associated with improved mental and physical health (Schorr, et. al., 2018). That is one reason why effective coaches sometimes have walking meetings in which the client is far away from interruptions and, with the benefit of some fresh air, can take a fresh look at their most vexing challenges.

FOCUS AND ORGANIZATIONAL HEALTH

Educational systems are by nature hierarchical bureaucracies. The farther away the level of decision-making is from the classroom, the more likely that the emphasis will be placed on strategies, plans, and the endless documents that accompany these requirements. But however seductive the lure of strategies and plans may be, the evidence favors focus over strategic planning (Goleman, 2013). In reaction to the voluminous documents that distract teachers and leaders from their primary mission, some schools have resolved to embrace the "plan on a page" (Reeves, 2020b), in which the mission, vision, values, and goals of a school are all on a single page. In contrast to the typical plan with a time horizon of three-to-five years, a growing number of schools and districts are changing the focus to 100 days—roughly a semester of 90 days along with ten days for planning and mid-course corrections (Reeves & Eaker, 2019). The emotional reactions to the vast majority of the long-term plans we have seen range from cynicism to despair, as the people in the classrooms and schools who must actually get the work done feel overwhelmed and frequently unheard. The reason for these reactions is that organizations are almost always better at adding new burdens for teachers and administrators than they are at removing the current initiatives, which demand all the time and attention of staff members. Fortunately, there is a way out of that organizational mess—the Garden Party.

THE POWER OF THE GARDEN PARTY AND THE NOT-TO-DO LIST

One of the most powerful interactions between coach and client is not the establishment of new programs and initiatives; rather, it is the process of explicitly removing some tasks, programs, and initiatives from the client's desk. In medical research, there is a process of de-implementation that takes place before any new therapies are added (Bauer, et. al., 2015). The coach-client relationship can be overwhelmed by the exigencies of the moment if both parties fail not only to carve out time for focusing on the coaching relationship but also to identify specific ways that the client can save time. The coach might begin with an initiative inventory, understanding every single task, program, and initiative that is on the client's desk. This includes not only obvious matters, such as curriculum and assessment, but also less obvious ways that time is lost, such as the overwhelming amount of electronic traffic that teachers and administrators receive. Coaches and clients should take care not to dismiss this focus on time as "mere management", when they wish to focus only on leadership. We must express the blunt truth that great leadership is not possible when the realities of time management, people management, and project management claim the vast majority of the day of school leaders. The simple discipline of responding to email three times a day rather than responding to each email and text as it comes in will dramatically improve the productivity of anyone, especially the very busy school leader (Newport, 2021).

Teachers want to improve their practice and provide the best possible support to students, but the most frequent barrier to these objectives is the consistent complaint, "We just don't have the time!" This is a challenge building administrators must confront directly. Some principals begin every semester with a garden party. The staff files into the meeting to see their leader dressed in overalls and a straw hat and notice a large waste basket with what appear to be paper weeds sprouting out of the top of the barrel. The meeting opens with the principal calling the attention of the staff to a date a month in the future. "Here she goes again," huffs the staff. "Another meeting." The principal then dramatically rips that page from her calendar and says, "Colleagues, that meeting is canceled because I want you to have time for collaborative scoring—" (or for formative assessment, or data analysis, or whatever necessary task for which no time has been allocated). "After all," the principal concludes, "we can't plant any flowers around here until we first pull the weeds." Polite applause may follow this announcement, as it is the first time in recent memory that the principal specifically removed something from the task lists of teachers.

The principal then lays down the challenge. "Friends, we all have weeds in our garden. There are curriculum weeds, transition weeds, bulletin board weeds, technology weeds, and many others. And think about weeds that we pull in our real gardens. They may be small, but they have deep roots and tend to keep coming back even after we have pulled them. So it requires constant vigilance on our part not only to pull the weeds but to keep them out of our classroom gardens." The principal concludes with some rules for the garden-weeding process. First, you must focus only on the weeds in your own garden—those you can control. Second, think small—saving a few minutes from every transition, for example, would save hours of precious instructional time every year. Rethinking the way that homework is assigned and graded, for example, having all the practice done in school rather than at home, could save teachers many hours while improving student learning.

* * *

In this chapter we have considered the imperative of focus for classroom educators, building leaders, and district administrators. The evidence of a commitment to focus is found in the specific tasks, programs, and initiatives that leaders and teachers will commit to stop doing. The most important focus is on student results and the actions of educators and leaders that are directly associated with improved results. Even if coaches are successful in helping clients pull some of their metaphorical weeds, the client and coach must also consider the psychological toll faced by educators and leaders every day. In the next chapter we will consider the reality of compassion-fatigue and how to deal with it.

QUESTIONS FOR REFLECTION:

1. What are the three top priorities for your role this year? If you could only succeed at three goals, what would they be?
2. What are three things you are willing to stop doing or, at the very least, have someone else—a student, assistant, paraprofessional—do?
3. Think of a colleague that has the same position you have. What advice would you give that colleague to gain focus by pulling some weeds? Why is it easier to see the weeds in other people's gardens than to see our own weeds?
4. Take a moment to look at your email inbox. Describe the feeling you would have if it were completely empty. What are some specific actions you can take today to move toward that empty inbox and the wonderful feelings that will inspire?

CHAPTER 10
AVOIDING INITIATIVE FATIGUE

- ❖ The Initiative Inventory
- ❖ Assessing Implementation
- ❖ Assessing Impact on Results
- ❖ Every Turkey Has a Champion

EVERY READER OF THIS BOOK IS PASSIONATE. WE ARE PASSIONATE about the needs of students and about our roles as educators who serve the needs of children every day. We are also passionate learners, excited to apply the latest and best evidence to our schools and classrooms. But while this passion inspires us in the bleakest of times, it can also be counterproductive, weighing us down under the avalanche of initiative fatigue. Our passion for the new often does not displace the passion for the old. And no amount of passion will grant us a 25-hour day. In this chapter, we consider how to channel our passion in the most effective manner and avoid passion fatigue.

THE INITIATIVE INVENTORY

Quick: How many instructional and leadership initiatives do you have right now? It's more than you think. When I posed this question to a senior administrator, a thoughtful and dedicated leader I have known for many years, he replied that he had only five priorities. He had, after all, read my research on the value of focus, and he was quite certain that his large, complex, urban district shared his focus on those five priorities. I replied respectfully, "Yes sir, but would you mind if I asked your teachers about that?" The teachers, who also loved and respected the leader, were clear in their assessment, listing more than 40 initiatives. They were overwhelmed and overloaded, even though the leader thought that the system was focused and had avoided initiative fatigue.

What causes initiative fatigue? It is possible that this is the result of senior leaders who buy one program after another, thinking that each new addition to the curriculum and schedule will solve their problems. Administrators are easy targets. But it is also possible that initiative fatigue is a result of classroom educators who are also enthusiastic about new ideas, yet who are unwilling to give up decades-old classroom activities and instructional units.

The first step in addressing this overload is the initiative inventory. This requires listing every instructional and leadership initiative at every level: classroom, school, district, state, federal, and grant provider. Whenever the clients say, "We don't have the time," the first step the Fearless Coach must take is to document an initiative inventory. The objective fact is that everyone on the planet has the same amount of time, so the only difference is not the number of hours in the day but the manner in which we choose to use those hours. Failure to conduct an initiative inventory is like the morbidly obese patient who, seeking the doctor's help, refuses to get on the scale and confront the essence of the challenge ahead.

My trainer, Elizabeth Sardine, who has been featured in *Boston* magazine as one of the most powerful women in our city and who specializes in helping people in middle age maintain healthy nutrition and exercise regimens, can divide her clients into two categories: those who are willing to weigh themselves and reveal their food consumption and those who are not. There is no fad diet, wardrobe strategy, or illusory self-talk that can take the place of objective data. Just as my trainer and her clients must address the brutal facts of weight, diet, and exercise—so also must the clients of Fearless Coaches address the brutal facts of student achievement, teaching practices, and leadership decisions.

ASSESSING IMPLEMENTATION

Once the initiative inventory has been conducted, the Fearless Coach must assist the client in assessing the degree of implementation of each initiative. Here is an abbreviated method for considering each level of implementation, although the details may differ from one initiative to another.

- Level 1: The materials were delivered. In Level 1 implementation, there are programs installed in the computers of teachers, boxes of curriculum and other materials delivered to the school, and other examples of mere delivery.
- Level 2: The teachers were trained. The fundamental misunderstanding about professional learning is that if teachers only knew the evidence and information, then they would change their practices.
- Level 3: There is evidence that teachers are applying this program in the classroom. For example, if the program is a writer's workshop, then there is evidence of student editing and rewriting. If the program involves cross-disciplinary writing, then there is evidence of student writing in subjects outside of English Language Arts.
- Level 4: There is evidence of an impact on student performance. For example, there is classroom-level data that shows "before and after" the implementation of the program. These

data could reflect student performance on assessments or actual examples of same-student-to-same-student writing and other performance assessment responses.

When the Fearless Coach has the initiative inventory and the level of implementation for every initiative in the school or district, then and only then can the coach provide the support and insight necessary to help clients achieve their personal and professional goals. At each meeting, the coach should ask, "Have you added any new initiatives since our last meeting? Have you terminated any initiatives?" When clients fail to accomplish their goals, it is almost never a lack of talent, desire, or personal commitment. It's a lack of focus. Clients devote time to easy things rather than challenging things.

This is certainly true of almost every writer I know, and it is especially true of people who want to become a writer without actually doing any writing. They will read, research, and think, but they have a very difficult time putting pen to paper or fingers to the keyboard and get the writing done.

In the case of the Fearless Coaching client, the failure to focus is the unending stream of distractions, from texts and emails to drop-ins to the office—to the latest crises of absent staff, unavailability of substitute teachers, late buses, and behavioral issues—all of which command the urgent attention of the leader. While the coach cannot dispense with these immediate demands for the attention of the leader, the coach can support the leader in making the transition from fixer to multiplier (Wiseman, 2010).

This is frustratingly difficult for leaders because they were promoted based on their ability to be a fixer. Everyone knows that Ellen can get the job done. She's reliable and trustworthy. Any problem—from a flat tire on the school bus to a problem in the cafeteria, to a colleague floundering with a class,—will gain Ellen's attention and she will fix it. The problem is that only Ellen can fix it. She is such a great fixer that no one else in the building dares to tackle these problems because everyone knows Ellen can do it better. Only after

Ellen is completely overwhelmed with overwork will the need for the transition to becoming a multiplier be clear.

ASSESSING IMPACT ON RESULTS

Avoiding initiative fatigue would be easy if all we had to do was do more of what works and less of what doesn't work. But how do you really know what works? Research, even that which claims to be "statistically significant", does not always help answer this question. The objections to research from working educators and administrators include, most commonly, that the students in the research were not representative of the students in their schools. They had different funding, a different union agreement, a different schedule, different leadership support, and a host of other variables that render the research irrelevant.

The research that is ultimately the most persuasive in creating sustainable change is the systematic comparison before and after an initiative is implemented. Systematic comparison means that the researcher is looking at the same teacher, same students, same curriculum, same assessments, same schedule, same funding, same union agreement, same everything. The only difference is the presence of the initiative—a teaching strategy, leadership decision, or other intervention. This evidence of change at the classroom and school level is exemplified in the "science fair" approach that we have found to be the best method of creating and sustaining change (Reeves, 2021a).

The science fair method of research looks just like it sounds, three-panel displays of the sort that students show in their science fairs. The three-panel displays show the direct experience of classroom teachers. The left-hand panel is the challenge. Perhaps it is excessive failures in ninth-grade math, chronic absenteeism in middle school, or behavioral disruptions in third grade. The middle panel shows the initiative, the specific professional practices of teachers and decisions of leaders. Examples include collaborative scoring of writing, technology-assisted geography instruction, math procedures drills, intensive phonics instruction, or any other explicit initiative that the teacher is using that is clearly different from past practice. The right side of the display contains the results. What was the difference from before the initiative was implemented to after it was created? When the students are all the same, along with every other variable that influences learning, then these before and after differences are almost certainly due to the implementation of the initiative. The period of time used for this analysis can be as short as six weeks (Hattie & Yates, 2014) to a semester or year. The key is that the teacher-researcher can confidently show the impact of the initiative. The demonstration of impact could be quantitative, such as the percentage of students who were proficient before and after the initiative. It could also be qualitative, such as the display of student work showing how the same student improved over time in writing, math problem-solving, scientific reasoning, or any other target of improvement.

The question *What works?* can lead to initiative fatigue because, as John Hattie has wryly noted, "Anything with a pulse works." Rather, the relevant questions are: *What works best?* and *What works here?* The only way to defeat initiative fatigue is the deliberate decisions of leaders at every level to stop the initiatives that are ineffective and wasteful. This can be a painful exercise. Principal Christine Brzeski in Greenfield, Wisconsin, has an annual "dumpster day" in which she helps teachers clear out decades-old word searches, bilious teachers-pay-teachers' worksheets, and aged instructional units carefully crafted during student teaching days but currently obsolete. She has tissues available, as parting with long-held activities is often a loss accompanied by tears. But it is necessary and the only way that this wonderful principal can fight initiative fatigue.

EVERY TURKEY HAS A CHAMPION

Wouldn't it be nice if solving initiative fatigue was met with a round of applause and a standing ovation? After all, everyone hates initiative fatigue, and we all agree that unnecessary, ineffective, and duplicative initiatives should be discarded, right? Well, not exactly. In our field research, we have found instances in which fewer than 1% of teachers are using an initiative. Terminating that initiative would save the district more than $100,000. So that should make us a hero, right? On the contrary, these demonstrably ineffective and unused initiatives have champions, the decision-makers who purchased the program and who are unable to give up on the belief that someday, somehow, the initiative will be effective. This is the sunk-cost fallacy in action (Kahneman, 2013). The job of the coach is to help the client distinguish between the original hope for an initiative and the present reality.

* * *

In this chapter we considered the challenge of initiative fatigue and how to fight it. Educators and leaders must first conduct an initiative inventory, identifying every instructional and leadership initiative that is part of the current agenda and those initiatives that have persisted over time from previous leaders. Each initiative can be assessed on four levels of implementation from delivery to training, to classroom implementation, to evidence of impact. We considered how inadequate traditional research is in creating change among educators and administrators and how the "science fair" approach—evidence of impact at the local level—is the best way to create and sustain change. These are the essential conversations in coaching teachers and principals. We now move to Part III, in which we consider how to coach teams.

QUESTIONS FOR REFLECTION:

1. What is your initiative inventory? Start alone and then compare notes with your colleagues. There are always more initiatives than you think.

2. How do you assess implementation? Think of a specific initiative that you have recently adopted in technology, curriculum, instruction, or assessment. What does great implementation look like? Write the characteristics of implementation alone and then compare with your colleagues. What are the similarities? What are the differences?
3. Think about an initiative that is failing. Is the problem the initiative itself or the implementation?

PART III
COACHING TEAMS

ALTHOUGH COACHING TEAMS IS MORE COMPLEX THAN COACHING individuals, we have found that team coaching is the most impactful coaching practice if the goal is improving student achievement. Schools around the world invest enormous amounts of time and money in collaborative teams, often under the banner of Professional Learning Communities or other popular labels. As Rick DuFour and I argued in "The Futility of PLC Lite", many of these investments are wasted due to lack of focus on the essentials of learning, assessment, support, enrichment, and the specific teaching practices that lead to improvement. We have seen collaborative team time devoted to bus schedules, field trips, discipline, and a variety of issues that are not related to teaching and learning. Team coaching can, within a matter of weeks, get these teams back on track. Moreover, when the coach provides explicit feedback to the teams and the school administrator, teachers and leaders save many hours by focusing on the essentials. Highly functional teams do not require administrative presence, save for brief affirmation. Struggling teams require the support of administrators in order to link actual team practices to idea practices.

In the chapters that follow, we consider both system-level teams, such as the cabinet and other central office teams, and school-based teams, such as leadership teams and collaborative teacher teams.

There is a significant research base that distinguishes the typical meeting—one person presents information while others glumly listen—and highly effective teams that are not only well-organized, but are also focused on deliberation and inquiry.

One of the most common complaints of teachers and administrators is the lack of time to achieve their goals. While we sympathize with this complaint, it is fundamentally inaccurate, as we all have the same amount of time. The question addressed in the following paragraphs is how we use the time that we have. In the vast majority of central office teams we have coached, we find that there are too many participants who are not engaged in the inquiry that an effective meeting should display, and we provide practical answers to balance the need for inclusion with the need for effective leadership. In teacher collaborative teams, we often find two extremes. The first is that the collaborative team is nothing more than a series of announcements—call it "Department Meeting 2.0". At the other extreme is, in an astonishing display of mistrust—45 minutes devoted to filling out paperwork for district and state administrators, without benefit of evidence, deliberation, and inquiry. In these chapters, we provide a balanced approach so that team members are appropriately accountable, but not micromanaged. Most importantly, we offer ideas that will save time for busy teachers and administrators.

CHAPTER 11
COACHING DISTRICT TEAMS AND SUPERINTENDENT'S CABINET

> ❖ The Value of Great Meetings
> ❖ The High Cost of Bad Meetings
> ❖ The Science of Effective Meetings
> ❖ Coaching Teams for Better Meetings

IN THIS CHAPTER WE EXPLORE THE OPPORTUNITIES AND COSTS OF meetings, with particular attention to senior leadership meetings. Some meetings are goal-oriented, clearly focused on a well-articulated challenge, and end with decisions that reflect the best available evidence. In these meetings, participants feel heard, divergent views are welcomed, and everyone leaves with a sense of accomplishment, knowing that the value of the meeting reflected their investment of time and intellectual energy. Few meetings at any level meet this vision of leadership excellence.

When the agenda (if there is one) is piled with reports that could have been emails, speakers engage in pontificating and verbal bomb-throwing. Then decisions are unclear, and participants leave demoralized and frustrated, uncertain as to why they invested two hours in yet another meeting without results, and often must hold a meeting after the meeting to try to learn what really happened. Some participants are there not because of their expertise or ability to make a contribution but merely to claim a place at the table, equating their prestige and power with proximity to senior leadership. These are the meetings that inspire the Despair.com poster that says of meetings: NONE OF US IS AS DUMB AS ALL OF US.

The guidelines in this chapter will allow you to have more meetings that are productive and fewer that go off the rails. And if even a well-planned meeting starts to become unproductive, you will have tools to call a time-out and get the meeting back on track. The role of the Fearless Coach is to hold a mirror up to the meeting participants and leaders so they can see themselves at their best as well as when they are less effective. The coaching role is essential because all the evidence and leadership theory in the world will not change existing unproductive meeting practices unless the leaders and participants in those meetings recognize the need to change. The coach does not tell the leader what to do but persistently asks the leaders about their frustrations with meetings and what they will commit to doing differently to address those concerns.

In the United States, private, governmental, nonprofit, and educational organizations spend more than a trillion dollars on meetings per year (Rogelberg, 2019). The financial cost, especially for senior leadership meetings, is extraordinary but rarely calculated. Time is a zero-sum game, and every hour devoted to meeting is an hour not devoted to mentoring new leaders, supporting parents and other stakeholders, collaborating with governing board members, and representing the school system to the community. Therefore, every meeting ought to begin with the question: Is what we are about to do more valuable than the other ways we could be spending our time—with colleagues, students, principals, and other stakeholders? If so, then the meeting has a significant opportunity for productivity and purpose—as opposed to when the most common response to the question, why do we have this meeting, is: "We have the meeting because it's Tuesday—that's when we always have this meeting." There is more than a financial cost to meetings, and that is the cost in morale, especially among our most overworked and highly stressed colleagues. When we consider why educators and administrators leave the profession, the answer, surprisingly, is not just money, but respect (Reeves, 2018). Every unproductive meeting sends, however unintentionally, the message that we don't respect the time of our colleagues.

THE VALUE OF GREAT MEETINGS

Although it can be tempting for leaders to simply cancel meetings, a better approach is to use the best evidence to make meetings more productive. University of North Carolina Management professor Steven Rogelberg has amassed evidence in *The Surprising Science of Meetings* that indicates that when organizations simply cancel meetings, believing that they are saving time, there are significant costs:

> Not holding enough meaningful meetings will likely derail employees, leaders, teams, and organizations. Holding too few meetings robs employees of essential information and feelings of inclusion, support, voice, and community.... Meetings foster commitment to goals and initiatives that connect jobs, as well as commitment to broader departmental and organizational aspirations that may not be explicitly stated in any individual job description.... In many ways, meetings are the building blocks and core elements of the organization: they are the venues where the organization comes to life for employees, teams, and leaders. (Rogelberg, 2019)

How do leaders bridge the gap between the reality of so many ineffective meetings and the promise of the great meetings that Rogelberg describes? The answer lies with scientific evidence, including laboratory studies of meetings, field studies, and experimental research. For example, meeting participants were assigned problems to solve in various meeting conditions, then the quality of their solutions was independently scored. These sorts of studies yield robust findings that allow leaders to use valuable meeting time to get real work done and minimize the time that many meetings consume on irrelevant and destructive grandstanding.

Well-run meetings can save money and time, accelerating communication, cutting through bureaucratic silos, and identifying the optimal solutions to complex problems. The challenge for the Fearless Coach is to compare the performance of the actual meetings to the best evidence-based practices in this chapter.

THE HIGH COST OF BAD MEETINGS

Bain consultants Michael Mankins and Eric Garton (2017) contend that the scarcest resources in organizations today are the time, talent, and energy of their people. Organizations squander these precious resources in "needless internal interactions, unproductive or inconsequential meetings, and unnecessary e-communications. The organization gets in the way of getting things done. Not many of us can generate great ideas when we are trapped in the thickets of meetings and bureaucratic procedures."

The leadership discipline essential to avoiding these toxic influences is focus, limiting meetings to inquiry, deliberation, and decision-making. Focus requires constraints on the items to be discussed as well as on the number of people at the table. Despite the efforts in many educational organizations to be broadly inclusive with cabinet meetings of one or two dozen participants, the impulse to inclusivity does not help team morale and can actively undermine it. The decisions made at the senior leadership level affect not only millions of dollars but also the educational opportunities for children and adults in the system. When a meeting is in essence an audience for a few people to address, frustration and rancor can set in. We see it in meetings when the majority of participants are consumed by emails and texts, trading chats with people inside and outside the meeting and otherwise disengaged in the decision-making process of the meeting. Worse yet, when team members see bad behavior such as sarcasm, irrelevant discussions—or just as toxic—stony silence, they accept this as the norm rather than what it is, unprofessional conduct that hurts the entire team.

In analyzing the relationship between organizational effectiveness and teams, Mankins and Garton concluded that the best employee benefit that A+ players can receive is the opportunity to work with other A+ players. In education, financial rewards are rare and often uniform, based more on years of service and degrees than on actual contributions to the mission. But the benefit leaders can provide that doesn't cost a cent is to respect people's time and focus meetings only on critical decisions and include only the people who can make substantive contributions to those decisions.

THE SCIENCE OF EFFECTIVE MEETINGS

The research on meetings is clear, but the application of the research remains rare. For example, here are ten key findings from the science of effective meetings:

1) Limit participation to no more than seven people. Past that critical number, fewer voices are heard and deep deliberation is less likely (Axtell, 2018). The reason that this rule is so often violated is the pressure on senior leaders to be inclusive, as if the purpose of meetings is Athenian democracy in which every citizen can vote. But that's an audience, not a meeting. If the purpose of the meeting is bringing creative solutions to complex challenges using the best available evidence, then focus, not broad inclusivity, is required.

2) Set and enforce norms. Norms can include: no cross-talk, no off-task use of technology, summarizing a previous speaker before

presenting an alternative viewpoint, reading meeting materials before the meeting, and backing up every assertion with evidence. The most effective meetings I have seen have an official norm minder, so the responsibility for norms is never left to the most senior person in the room or to the meeting facilitator but is widely shared by all participants.

3) Forget traditional brainstorming. The widely used and thoroughly discredited tradition of brainstorming stems from the evidence-free writings of an advertising executive in the 1940s by the name of Alex Osborn (1953). You have doubtless participated in one of these sessions in which the enthusiastic facilitators announce that no idea is bad and whatever you do, don't judge the ideas. This is terrible advice. There is an evidence-based approach to creativity and brainstorming, but it involves the opposite of Osborn's 70-year-old suggestions. MIT researchers found that if the objective of the brainstorming suggestion is the creation of innovative solutions that have value to the organization and can be recalled by the participants in the meeting, then the process begins not with a group of people throwing out ideas; rather, it begins with each member working alone to generate possible solutions, followed by a process that encourages debate and evaluation (Gregersen, 2018).

4) Clarify decision roles. Some decisions require consensus, other might be a majority rule, and still others are the exclusive prerogative of the leader. It is essential that the decision-making structure is clear before deliberation begins. Too often, meeting leaders convey the impression that they want input from everyone in the room, but the people in the meeting assume that a leader valuing their input means that the leader will agree with them. Most team members can handle the boss disagreeing with their perspective, but they need to know in advance what the decision-making structure is. Other roles might involve specific expertise, such as legal matters or technology constraints. While the general counsel and technology director may not be the final decision-makers, they

have an affirmative obligation to share their expertise about potential obstacles to effective implementation of a decision.

5) Articulate decisions clearly and check for understanding. Every classroom educator has had the experience of asking if anyone has questions, and hearing none, makes the misguided assumption that the lesson was clear and the students all understood what the teacher was saying. Wise teachers always have meaningful checks for understanding and never assume that silence means understanding. Similarly, in effective senior leadership meetings, decisions are recorded not just in minutes, but clearly displayed on a screen in real time so that each participant can review, ask questions, and gain clarification.

6) Establish a charter. Every cabinet, standing committee, and task force should have a charter that establishes the purpose of the meeting and the norms to be followed. For example, a cabinet charter might be something like this:

> The purpose of the cabinet is to support optimal decision-making by the superintendent and governing board through evidence-based deliberation. Every cabinet member is responsible for careful consideration of the evidence for and against decision alternatives before the meeting, and for coming to the meeting prepared to ask questions and make cogent arguments for and against the alternative decisions.

Note what this charter does not include: updates, PowerPoint presentations, and information-sharing, all of which should be presented through memoranda before the meeting, not by oral reports to the cabinet. Proposed agenda items that do not conform to the charter can be reviewed before the meeting and either eliminated or revised.

7) Require evidence that is clear, transparent, and traceable. "People are saying" is the phrase used by advocates for a position that is unsupported by evidence. Cabinet members must ask, "Who exactly is saying this, and what evidence do they have to support the claim?" Unfortunately, such a question can be interpreted as reflecting a lack of trust in a colleague and an unproductive conversation ensues:

"What's the matter, don't you trust me?"

"Of course I trust you, but I need to see the evidence before supporting this decision."

"Look, the evidence is my thirty-two years of experience in this system."

"No one doubts your experience or trustworthiness, but it's essential that our decisions are supported by evidence."

"Well, it sure sounds like distrust to me."

This entire argument could have been avoided if there were a norm about the use of clear, transparent, and traceable evidence. Students who write essays are required to support their viewpoints with evidence and examples and then offer clear citations of their sources. Surely, we should expect the same of cabinet officers.

8) Insist on mutually exclusive decision alternatives. The typical decision-making protocol for superintendents and governing boards is for the staff to make a recommendation and request the adoption of a single alternative. This process provides the illusion of unanimity and shields the superintendent and board from some of the most important elements of the decision-making process—the consideration of alternatives, along with the advantages and disadvantages of each.

Rather than bringing a single recommendation to the CEO on difficult issues, the staff should have at least two alternatives that are mutually exclusive, and each accompanied by advantages and disadvantages. The cabinet would serve the district better if, before the meeting, each member read and thought about a crisp memorandum— no longer than one or two pages—that had decision recommendations with advantages and disadvantages. There are *always* disadvantages and risks to every alternative. Leaders never make perfect decisions; rather, they choose thoughtfully among alternative risks. The vast majority of senior administrators I know are not accustomed to the consideration of alternatives, because that requires disagreement among the cabinet members. Brainwashed into the need for "buy-in", participants submerge disagreement behind a façade of gentility. Consider for a moment, however, a decision that with the benefit of hindsight, you now know was a bad one. Perhaps it was a technology acquisition, instructional initiative, or hiring decision. Would the bad decision have been avoided, or at least modified, if you had had at least one clear alternative and if the cabinet had had a clear-eyed view of the advantages and disadvantages of the decision that it made?

The discipline of mutually exclusive decision alternatives is especially important when committees or task forces make recommendations to the cabinet. When only a single alternative is presented, it is difficult for the superintendent to do anything but accept the apparently unanimous recommendation of the group. We must remember, however, that these recommendations are rarely unanimous and, if they were, it is most likely evidence that there was insufficient exploration of alternatives and inadequate consideration of advantages and disadvantages.

9) Say it once—*but say it*. At the conclusion of each deliberation, the leader of the meeting should give each member the opportunity to offer observations, affirmations, or reservations. While this is not the time to repeat arguments, it is essential that each member respond to the question: "Is anything left unsaid?" The requirement is that you either say it in the meeting and get it resolved, or the matter is over. The price of membership in the cabinet is candor. When arguments are held behind closed doors, in the hallways, or parking lot, then the cabinet and superintendent are shut out of essential deliberations.

10) Establish the cabinet as the face of the system. In every cabinet meeting I have observed, there are some members who check out, not because of a lack of interest but because the norm has been established that they only participate in matters that pertain to their area of expertise. Thus, the cabinet members responsible for facilities and finance rarely ask questions about curriculum and instruction, and vice versa. This is wrong-headed on two counts. First, when members of the community encounter someone who has the rank of assistant superintendent, they assume that this person represents the entire school system. If the community is skeptical about a new bond issue or new grading system, it won't do for them to hear from a top district official, "Sorry, that's not my responsibility." The people who vote for and against facilities referenda, for and against ballot measures that directly affect educational policies and resources, and for and against board members, have a right to be informed in a thoughtful and practical way. Second, there is enormous value to the decision-making process when a cabinet member asks deliberately naïve questions:

- "I know I'm not an expert in curriculum and assessment, but I really don't understand the rationale for the math curriculum you are suggesting."
- "You can take everything I know about technology and put it in a very small bag, but I'd appreciate it if you would explain how this proposed program will improve the quality of teaching and learning in our system. If I can't understand it, then I suspect there are many other staff members who will have a hard time with it as well."
- "I know that this new employee benefit system is supposed to be a motivating reward, but I just don't see how it helps my administrative team. Please walk me through it so that this becomes a motivator and not a burden."

COACHING TEAMS FOR BETTER MEETINGS

When the Fearless Coach is meeting with an individual leader, the focus is on the personal and professional goals of the client. This focus shifts when the client is no longer an individual but a team. The question is not merely what best suits the individual—rather, what is best for the organization. We have found that even when there are reams of paper with plans, visions, mission statements, needs analyses, and strategies—it is often not sufficient to get a clear response to the simple question: What is the shared goal that we all have in common? Earlier, we used the metaphor of the mirror in which the coach provides clear and objective feedback to the team. This is not about what the coach liked or didn't like, but purely objective observation. Examples include:

- "I noticed that Ellen did not comment on six of the seven agenda items."
- "When the new curriculum was proposed, there was no alternative provided for the group to consider."
- "When Tom made a budget recommendation based on what he said was common practice in our region, no one asked Tom for elaboration or evidence."
- "When Mary began her PowerPoint presentation, no one addressed the norm that all materials were to be shared before the meeting and that the purpose of the meeting was deliberation, not presentation."
- "When the discussion got heated at one point, I noticed that Franklin asked for a time-out to think and reflect."

The Fearless Coach is not the judge or evaluator but an objective observer. Given the potential positive impact of great team meetings and bad meetings' potential negative impact on morale, productivity, and effective decision-making—this sort of feedback is essential. When the auditors review the financial records of a district, they don't say what they liked or didn't like. They just report the facts.

Because they support senior leadership teams at the district level, this is precisely what Fearless Coaches must do. In the following chapter, we will consider coaching teams at the school level.

**

In this chapter we considered the challenges and rewards of senior leadership team meetings. Next, in Chapter 12 we will apply these lessons to meetings at the school level, including school leadership teams and meetings of teacher teams.

QUESTIONS FOR REFLECTION:

1. Consider the last leadership team meeting you observed. Compare your observations to the elements of effective meetings in this chapter. How many participants were there? To what extent was the meeting focused on deliberation and inquiry rather than presentations? To what degree were the participants prepared by reading and thinking about the materials provided before the meeting? To what degree did participants adhere to meeting norms?
2. Think about an upcoming leadership meeting. Based on what you learned in this chapter, what specific steps can you take to make that a more productive use of everyone's time?
3. If your next meeting does not have a charter, what would you propose as a draft charter for the team to consider?

CHAPTER 12

COACHING SCHOOL LEADERSHIP TEAMS AND TEACHER TEAMS

- ❖ The Collaboration Imperative
- ❖ Focus on Learning, Teaching, and Leadership
- ❖ Saving Time with Four-line Emails
- ❖ Coaching Teacher and Administrator Teams

IN THE LAST CHAPTER, WE CONSIDERED THE UNIQUE NEEDS OF DIStrict-level leadership teams and provided guidelines for keeping those teams focused on the most important work. We also considered some of the evidence-based practices for effective meetings. Most importantly, we defined the purpose of meetings as deliberation, inquiry, and decision-making, not presentations or announcements. Those guidelines are also apt for teams at the school level, including building administrators and classroom educators. In the daily lives of principals and teachers, there is no time to waste. In this chapter we consider how to make the most of collaborative time in order to have the greatest impact on learning, teaching, and leadership.

THE COLLABORATION IMPERATIVE

In synthesizing more than two decades of research on leadership practices that have the greatest impact on student results, a study commissioned by the Wallace Foundation (Grissom, et. al., 2021) found that one of the keys to effective leadership is fostering a climate of collaboration among teachers and administrators. While many schools have scheduled time for "Professional Learning Communities" and other collaborative team time, the degree of effectiveness of these teams varies wildly, from high-impact teams to what can best be described as "PLC Lite" (DuFour & Reeves, 2016). While the effectiveness of the classroom teacher is the top influence on student achievement, the ability of classroom teachers to be effective on the job and to be motivated to remain in the profession is largely the responsibility of building leadership.

Using the coaching and observation tools in the Appendix, we have seen building-level teams transform from an audience sullenly listening to announcements to vibrant and engaged teams who understand deeply the student learning that needs to take place, the data that shows the difference between the desired learning and the current state of student learning, specific teaching interventions that make immediate improvements in student learning, and enrichment activities to engage and inspire students who are already meeting learning expectations.

While many excellent teachers have been able to accomplish these objectives alone, the power of collaboration is the key to having school-wide and system-level results. While a single teacher can be unquestionably masterful as a professional, the impact of that mastery can be diluted quickly in the absence of effective collaborative teams. The essence of this change is the move from private practice, the solo practitioner doing a fine job independently—to public practice, the team of teachers and administrators committed to school-wide improvement (DuFour, et. al., 2006).

This commitment to success beyond the walls of a single classroom requires a spirit of collective responsibility for all students.

Moreover, it requires professionals at every stage of their career to engage in continuous learning, acceptance of alternative methods to succeed with difficult challenges, and an obligation to share one's own most effective practices with colleagues. Collaboration does not happen naturally. Educators are accustomed to being masters of their domain and experts in their field. In many schools, it is unusual and uncomfortable to be in a team meeting that suggests that even experts can improve performance. Thus, it requires not only supreme professional confidence to engage in effective collaboration but also a high degree of trust in colleagues and leadership. This sort of fearlessness is essential for learning by students and every staff member (Edmondson, 2018; Reeves, 2023).

FOCUS ON LEARNING, TEACHING, AND LEADERSHIP

In an effective school-level team meeting, there are only four agenda items. Each of these items ends with a question mark, inviting deliberation and inquiry. They do not end in a period, suggesting that one person is making a presentation while others are passively listening. These are the four questions:

1. What do we want students to learn?
2. How will we know if they have learned it?
3. What will we do if they have not learned it?
4. What will we do if they already have learned it? (DuFour, et. al., 2006).

Even with 45 minutes to invest in collaboration, it takes an exceedingly well-disciplined team to address these four questions. We would acknowledge that a very successful meeting might consider only one of the questions to give it the full depth of consideration that it deserves. However, if the only thing that a team does is the first question—laboring over units, lesson plans, and the subjects to be addressed—and they never get to the other three questions, then their collaborative efforts will have little impact.

Despite the primacy of these four questions, we continue to witness team meetings that include: announcements that could have been in emails; two-person conversations that wasted the time of the entire group; and presentations, sometimes with PowerPoint slides taken from a workshop—all mere information-sharing that could have been provided in writing. Collaboration is imperative for improved learning, teaching, and leadership, and collaboration never happens in a meeting dominated by one person talking and everyone else listening.

The third question, "What do we do if students have not learned it," is often misunderstood and sometimes leads to the referral of students to special education or pull-out intervention programs. The remedy for students who do not learn something the first time, however, is not this sort of intervention, but rather effective instruction. When students do not learn something immediately, it is neither a calamity nor a cause for labeling the student. It's just another regular day at school when students need support and effective instruction in order to master the academic challenges they face.

SAVING TIME WITH FOUR-LINE EMAILS

One of the greatest concerns of teachers is time: too much curriculum, too many assessments, too many students, and not enough time to deal with the demands of their jobs. One of the best ways to start a conversation with busy classroom educators is the promise that this idea will save time, not cost them extra minutes they do not have.

In any complex organization, such as a school or district, there will always be variation in the degree of implementation of any professional practice. Even when teachers and administrators have had the same professional learning, the same schedule allowing time for collaboration, and the same guidelines for how to conduct effective meetings, variations in the quality of impact of these meetings will persist. In schools, the antidote to this variation has been ill-fated attempts at micromanagement in which teams of teachers devote all their collaboration time to filling out forms and worksheets designed to provide accountability to a higher headquarters. In smaller schools, the principal may make an effort to be personally present in every team meeting, attempting to provide a degree of consistency in the conduct of the meetings. But neither micromanagement through laborious documentation nor intensive supervision provide long-term answers to the need for effective collaboration. What is needed is a balance of accountability and autonomy, and for that we suggest the four-line email that corresponds to the four questions listed above. The lines on the email are:

1. Learning
2. Assessment
3. Support
4. Enrichment

These are short, can be done in the last two minutes of the meeting and shared with all meeting participants to ensure that this simple four-line email accurately reflects what the collaborative team did. It provides immediate accountability to building or district administrators on the essence of what was accomplished, and not accomplished, in these meetings. In some meetings, perhaps the only emphasis was on assessment. So, lines 1, 3, and 4 are left blank. That is very valuable data for school leaders to have. If after a month of meetings, a team is never addressing enrichment, then that suggests a need for greater support.

Here is an example of the four-line email from a third-grade team. In this example, the team did not discuss everything they were doing—just a particular concern that all teachers on the team shared—adding and subtracting fractions with unlike denominators. There are data from a common formative assessment, not just their personal impressions, that told them this was an essential area of focus. Note that we emphatically do not recommend that someone take minutes of these meetings, because that takes one person out of the discussion, and no administrator we know has the time to read the minutes, anyway. The team just focused on the essentials of the four-line email:

1. Learning: Math unit on fractions with denominators 2, 3, 4, 6, and 8.
2. Assessment: On a 10-item quiz on adding fractions, fewer than 70% of students scored 8 out of 10 or higher. The most frequently missed quiz items were with the denominators of 3 and 8.
3. Support: We created 15-minute mini-lessons on fractions, including both manipulatives (parts to whole), followed by two-item sample quiz items. We will do this for the next five instructional days.
4. Enrichment: The 30% of students who scored 80% or higher will use mini-lesson time to create story problems illustrating practical use of the items in the fractions test. If time permits, they will also tackle three- and four-fraction addition problems with unlike denominators, such as 1/2 + 1/4 + 1/8 = ?

That's it. No announcements. No field trip discussion. No complaints about parents, discipline, politicians, or administrators. Just learning, assessment, support, and enrichment.

School and district leaders can easily synthesize these four-line emails to determine if there are some questions that are receiving inadequate attention for the school and district overall. For example, our experience is that the greatest amount of attention is devoted to the first question: what students are expected to learn. The development and collaborative scoring of common formative assessments is at the heart of the second question. The third question, support for students who have not yet achieved proficiency, requires particular attention. Indeed, the term "support" itself can lead to confusion, because in the eyes of some teachers and administrators, this implies a referral for special education. That is absolutely not our intent. When students are having difficulty in meeting a learning expectation, such as 70%

of the third-grade students in the example above in learning fraction operations, it's not a sign of a disability. Rather, the students need immediate and intensive in-class support to build the specific skills that they need. Enrichment is the least answered question, especially in high-poverty schools. When so many students are struggling to meet basic academic requirements, it is easy to overlook that there are almost always students who are succeeding and, without explicit enrichment activities, can become bored, distracted, and act out in unhelpful ways.

The four-line email saves time for teachers in collaborative teams, avoids micromanagement that stems from bureaucratic forms, and allows leadership teams at all levels to identify successes and challenges that must be addressed.

COACHING TEACHER AND ADMINISTRATOR TEAMS

As with district-level leadership teams, the role of the coach is not to manage the team or give them advice on what to do; rather, it is to provide objective feedback on what the team is really doing and compare that to what the team aspires to do. One way that Fearless Coaches provide feedback to teams is using a scoring guide, the Leading Collaborative Teams of Teachers and Administrators Checklist, which is provided as Appendix F and downloadable at https://www.creativeleadership.net/fearless-books. The coach provides feedback on each of the following five dimensions:

1. Meeting Norms and Roles of Team Members
2. Identification of Learning Intentions and Tier-1 Instruction
3. Evidence of Student Understanding
4. Team Planning for Intervention and Enrichment Activities
5. Team Reporting/Feedback

Each dimension is scored on a four-point scale, from emerging to mastery, and space is provided for the coach to provide specific observations.

* * *

We now turn our attention to Part IV, providing feedback for improved results. This is the most difficult and most important role of the coach. We naturally value a good relationship with clients, and they depend on our honesty and candor. If a coaching relationship depends solely on affirmation and feel-good pabulum, then the clients will not achieve the results they and their schools need.

QUESTIONS FOR REFLECTION:

1. Consider the most recent collaborative team meeting you have observed. What were the main topics of conversation? What elements of the four questions of a Professional Learning Community were addressed, and which questions were omitted?
2. When you consider the four main topics of a collaborative team meeting: learning, assessment, support, and enrichment—which questions are your colleagues most reluctant to address? What do you think are the barriers to those discussions?
3. Think of a collaborative team that has made great progress in identifying effective practices and improving teaching and learning. What caused that team to make progress?
4. Think of a team that is stuck and apparently unable or unwilling to make progress in improved teaching and learning. What are the reasons in your judgment that the team is stuck, and how can you use what you have learned in this chapter to help that team improve?

PART IV
RESULTS: REAL-TIME FEEDBACK FOR CONTINUAL ENERGY AND ENTHUSIASM

IN THE NEXT CHAPTERS WE CONSIDER THE RELATIONSHIP BETWEEN the causes of student achievement (effective teaching and leadership) and the effects (measurable gains in student achievement). There is certainly no shortage of measurable results in schools, as teachers and students strain under a growing number of tests designed to give teachers, leaders, and the public information about student performance. The challenge is not a lack of measurement but the failure to measure what matters most. The greatest gap in measurement is not tests of student performance but measurement of the underlying causes—what teachers and leaders do to cause results. That is the heart of Chapter 14, a review of leading indicators of student success. Coaches in particular must focus not merely on the data from tests of student performance but on the less frequently measured actions of teachers and leaders as well. While nearly every school administrator claims to be looking at data, it is far rarer for them to link this information to what teachers and school leaders are doing and failing to do. Part IV concludes with a consideration of leadership in times of crisis and how the coach can synthesize all of these lessons to provide optimal support for clients.

CHAPTER 13

MEASURING WHAT MATTERS MOST

> ❖ Balancing Causes and Effects
> ❖ The Primacy of Adult Actions
> ❖ Coaching for Results

AT THE HEART OF FEARLESS COACHING IS THE MUTUAL COMMITment of the client and coach to pursue and achieve personal and professional goals. The only way that everyone involved, including not only the coach and client but also the many stakeholders whose success depends on the success of the leader, can know if there has been progress toward the goals is the accurate and timely measurement of results. While almost every school and district claim to be "data-driven", in the vast majority of instances we have observed, the data on which leaders rely to measure progress are late, ambiguous, inconsistently gathered, and often unrelated to the stated goals of the leader. In this chapter we consider not merely how to measure results, but more importantly, how to measure what matters.

BALANCING CAUSES AND EFFECTS

When most leaders talk about results, they are usually referring to student test scores, surveys of employee and student engagement, parent satisfaction, votes on bond issues, the number of discipline infractions, and other objectively measurable data. What all these measures have in common is that they are focused exclusively on effects, not causes. The leader will know that test scores rose or fell but have not a clue about the teaching and leadership decisions that caused those changes. This leads to one of two unfortunate conclusions. When I ask, for example, why seventh-grade math scores are down, the leaders might speculate that due to the high numbers of students in poverty or the number of English learners, these demographic characteristics must be at the root cause of low performance. Phrases such as "our demographics" are regularly infused into conversations about student performance, a phrase that is very convenient because leaders are unable to change family income, the language spoken at home, or the students' ethnic heritage. This is what Martin Seligman, University of Pennsylvania professor, former president of the American Psychological Association, and founder of the Positive Psychology movement calls, "learned helplessness" (Seligman, 2006).

When leaders and educators believe that the factors that most influence student performance are outside their realm of control or influence, then poor performance becomes a self-fulfilling prophecy. These perceptions of helplessness, together with a lack of efficacy by the professionals in the building, are strongly linked to lower student performance; higher levels of efficacy, by contrast, are strongly associated with improved student performance. But we will never unlock the keys to teacher and leader efficacy with data, workshops, speeches, and books on the subject (Guskey, 2021).

The only way to build the sense of control and perception of efficacy—learned optimism rather than learned helplessness—is for leaders to explicitly link the results they seek to achieve with the underlying causes. There is overwhelming data that poverty has an adverse impact on student achievement, and equally overwhelming research that shows that students in high-poverty schools can be successful (Chenoweth, 2017, 2020; Reeves, 2020a). Leaders can look at specific teaching and leadership actions that are strongly associated with high performance in high-poverty schools. These cause variables include, for example, collaborative scoring of student work, nonfiction writing in every subject, and an explicit commitment by teams of teachers to compare both their results and their teaching practices in a continual search for the most effective methods to help their students learn.

A systematic study of causes that lead to results takes the coaching discussions out of the realm of speculation and victim-blaming into the realm of thoughtful analysis and the consequent potential for constructive leadership decisions. After the school closures associated with the COVID pandemic, many students were significantly behind in their learning of grade-level skills (Kuhnfeld & Tarasawa, 2020). Debates on the semantics of the matter are unhelpful, as some leaders resolutely refuse to look at data that students are a year or more behind in meeting reading and math requirements—yet avoid the term "learning loss".

Whatever we call it, there is in many schools—before and after the COVID-related school closures—a clear need for direct intervention to support student reading and math skills. Although billions of dollars were provided to school districts by the federal government in COVID-relief funds, the acid test question for leaders is this: Now that you know that students have exceptional learning needs, how will your schedule, time allocation, curriculum, assessment, and teaching practices be different? In an astonishing number of cases, the answer is that there are no differences. Students were behind before COVID, they remain behind in the years after COVID, and we are not going to change anything. There are no guaranteed cures for alcohol and drug addiction, but it is certain that the ingestion of more alcohol and drugs is not the cure. The resolute commitment to engage in the same practices and decisions that led to poor results is neither the product of a truly results-driven leader nor is it an acceptable outcome of Fearless Coaching. One of the first actions that the coach must ask is, "If you want to change your results, are you willing to make changes in the causes that lead to these results—that is, are you willing to make changes in teaching and leadership?" The most resilient schools are those with leaders who are willing to embrace necessary change.

The good news is that we have seen schools embrace a focus on causes, not just effects, with remarkable results. For example, in one large high-poverty high school in California, failures in math and science decreased by more than 80% when teachers who assumed that a practice was happening at home deliberately shifted to performing that practice during class periods. They also shifted from calculating semester grades based on the average of student performance throughout the semester to evaluating students based on their achievement of state standards. We have seen similar results around the nation in which deliberate actions by teachers to improve the quality of practice and the accuracy of grading led to fewer failures, better discipline, fewer repeaters, fewer dropouts, more electives, and a better school climate and culture that benefitted all students and staff members. This did not occur as a result of an administrative mandate but because teachers systematically analyzed the causes of low performance, changed their practices to address those causes, and then publicly shared their results with the entire system (Reeves, 2019).

THE PRIMACY OF ADULT ACTIONS

Even very high-functioning teams of teachers and administrators are consistently better at analyzing student data than at considering the adult actions that are the underlying causes of student results. Leaders must ask questions like these:

- How could I do a more effective job of classroom observations and providing feedback to teachers?
- How could I change the schedule to give teachers and students the time they need to gain proficiency on essential skills?

- How can I accelerate the flow of information, so that if a student needs assistance, the student receives that support well before failing a class?
- How can I systematically identify and replicate the most effective teaching practices in the school?

Teachers must ask:

- What differences do I notice between students whose academic performance, engagement, and behavior are significantly better than other groups? To what extent do my teaching practices account for some of these differences?
- Who are my colleagues who appear to be achieving significantly better results with some of the students who are struggling in my class?
- What clues can I gather from conversations with my students about what activities are most or least engaging in my classroom?

COACHING FOR RESULTS

In our collective observations of thousands of meetings of teachers and administrators, we find that the discussions of student data are far more common than discussions of how the actions of those teachers and leaders directly relate to student data. In order to change that situation, coaches must engage in a persistent pattern of inquiry, always asking: "What do you think caused these results?" and "What do you think you could do to influence these results?" These questions are at the heart of collective efficacy in a school. As leaders observe team meetings and review the notes—the four-line emails to which we referred earlier—they must ask what the information about student achievement implies for specific actions in teaching and leadership.

Coaches can be especially helpful in identifying specific ways to measure adult actions. Examples of measuring what matters include the following:

- Percentage of lesson plans that include very brief preassessment as a daily activity, so that teachers avoid wasting time on lessons for which students need foundational skills
- Percentage of classes outside of English language arts that include requirements for nonfiction writing at least once per month
- Percentage of classes that include common formative assessments with collaborative scoring
- Percentage of school schedules that reflect an explicit recognition of student learning needs and show modification of time allocation to support student needs
- Percentage of collaborative team meetings that include explicit relationship between student results and adult actions of teachers and leaders
- Percentage of classroom observations in which there was 100% student engagement
- Percentage of classrooms in which teachers used best practices for student engagement, such as equity sticks or random calling
- Percentage of staff meetings devoted to deliberation and inquiry that avoided announcements and presentations that could have been presented in written form outside of the meeting

Perhaps some of these ideas seem so obvious that the use of a coach to identify and measure them seems unnecessary. But there is a yawning gap between what we know should be done and the actual practices in schools. The coach is not the judge or evaluator but is there to simply tell the truth, holding a mirror to the staff and allowing them to see their professional practices as they are, not as they wish they were. While staff members are accustomed to assigning numerical values to student performance, they tend to take a more ambiguous approach to adult actions. We are understandably enthusiastic about teacher creativity and inspirational leadership, factors that do not seem to be amenable to quantification. Although the coach can and should encourage these qualities, it is also essential for the coach to help clients set objectively measurable goals for improved teaching and leadership practices.

***

In this chapter we considered the challenge of measuring what matters most, balancing student results with the need to assess in specific terms the actions of teachers and leaders. In the next chapter we consider the vitally important topic of leading indicators. This is the area where the Fearless Coach can have the greatest impact on improved student results through rigorous and objective feedback on teaching and leadership.

QUESTIONS FOR REFLECTION:

1. Think of a particular element of teaching or leadership that you know is important, but you have had difficulty in measuring. How might you make that important action subject to an objectively measurable observation?
2. Consider a specific teaching or leadership action that you know is important, but you have had difficulty putting into action. What are the barriers to more effective implementation of these practices? What is a baseline measurement you could use to start making progress in improving these actions?
3. What are the sources of resistance to measuring adult actions in your school or district? How can you more effectively distinguish feedback on improved teaching and leadership from formal evaluation?
4. What are the similarities and differences between your formal evaluation system and what you have learned in this chapter about objective feedback?

CHAPTER 14

LEADING INDICATORS

- ❖ Focused Leadership
- ❖ Effective Classroom Instruction
- ❖ Accurate Feedback for Students
- ❖ Deliberate Practice for Students and Staff
- ❖ Laser-like Focus on Achievement
- ❖ Collaborative Scoring
- ❖ Comprehensive Nonfiction Writing
- ❖ Explicit Instructional Leadership

WHEN EDUCATIONAL LEADERS AND POLICYMAKERS TALK ABOUT ACcountability, they tend to emphasize a single word: results. This is understandable, as clear and measurable results are the key to guiding any organization in any field. Whether the result desired is student achievement, attendance, donations to a nonprofit organization, weight loss for prediabetic patients, or sales for a business, results are what drive the organization. However, the thesis of this chapter is a consideration of results that neglects that the underlying causes of those results—what this chapter refers to as the leading indicators—can lead to misleading interpretations and disastrous consequences. The business leaders who focus only on revenues, but ignore the source of those revenues, will be unable to determine if the revenues are sustainable—the product of systematic marketing and relationship building—or are idiosyncratic events that are not replicable.

The physician and patient who focus only on weight loss need to know if the cause of the weight loss is diet and exercise or an eating disorder, drug abuse, or serious illness. This is especially important for parents of teens who, unwisely, believe that they must constantly be on a diet to be healthy or at least sufficiently attractive to fit in with their critical peers. If all patients and their parents observe are the results—the reading on the scale—then they risk an unhealthy obsession with weight at the expense of overall health (Family Education, 2019). Similarly, when educators and school leaders focus only on student results—typically test scores, attendance, and discipline records—they risk failing to understand the underlying causes of those results, and that failure impedes their ability to improve student outcomes.

In this chapter, we explore these cause variables, the leading indicators of student achievement. We begin with a consideration of leadership focus, an essential and easy-to-observe leading indicator. One can simply count the number of priorities that are reflected in a school or district plan to assess their degree of focus and, as Michael Fullan has wryly observed, the number of priorities is inversely proportional to gains in student achievement (Reeves, 2013). While leaders and policymakers are often seduced by the promises of vendors that a program will solve every educational challenge, the evidence is clear that it is practices, not programs, that have the greatest impact. Almost every reader of this book has witnessed the phenomenon of a same program with identical training, components, and delivery yielding vastly different results because of different levels of implementation.

Next, we turn our attention to effective classroom instruction, by far the greatest single impact on student achievement (Hattie & Yates, 2014). This emphasis on effective instruction is at the heart of effective leadership coaching. Any educational leadership coaching worthy of the name must focus relentlessly on effective instruction, and we will consider a simplified approach to help leaders, instructional coaches, peer coaches, and classroom educators focus on the essentials.

Alongside effective instruction is the imperative of accurate and specific feedback. As a leading indicator, feedback is a powerful predictor of improved student results if (and only if) that feedback is directly related to student performance and delivered with sufficient specificity and timeliness to influence student performance. Sadly, much of the feedback provided to students—from homework papers to test performance—fails to meet these standards of specificity and timeliness. Students get a score, someday, but do not use that information to improve their performance.

Deliberate practice is another key leading indicator, and one that can be observed in every classroom. It is common in the music studio and athletic field but regrettably uncommon in the classroom. This sort of practice is difficult, requiring students to work outside of their comfort zone, like the high jumper who sets the bar progressively higher than the last successful jump rather than repeating the already mastered successful height. Deliberate practice is a progressive set of challenges that are personalized and difficult but ultimately rewarding as they lead to success.

The next leading indicator is the laser-like focus on achievement, an indicator reflected in the casual conversations of teachers, the agendas of staff meetings, and the physical artifacts in the building, such as the trophy case. Collaborative scoring, an objectively measurable practice that is strongly associated with improved student results, follows. The reason that collaborative scoring is so important is that it transforms standards and curriculum into the explicit expectations for student work.

Finally, we consider the imperative of explicit instructional leadership. The leading indicator is not only the degree to which leaders know what effective instruction is but also the frequency with which they are actively observing classrooms and providing explicit feedback to teachers.

FOCUSED LEADERSHIP

No matter how generous the budget or flexible the schedule, every school is bound by the same constraint: time. A billion-dollar grant will not buy a 25-hour day. Therefore, one of the most important supports that a coach provides is focus. When leaders face myriad demands on their time and attention, focus may seem elusive. Some of the fragmentation that is the enemy of focus is institutional—the forms, reports, and meetings that other levels of the organization require. Other sources of fragmentation are self-imposed, such as the common practice of responding to every visual and auditory cue from electronic devices, causing constant switching between tasks and areas of mental focus.

Georgetown computer science professor Cal Newport (2021) has amassed significant evidence that fragmented attention, especially among knowledge workers (the description of everyone in education), has caused dramatic declines in productivity and focus. For example, we check email on average every six minutes, and every shift in task takes up to 20 minutes to successfully refocus our mental energy. When leaders are focused, they resist the illusion of service associated with immediate response to every text and email and give their colleagues, students, and schools the benefit of their full attention. This means, for example, that they answer email three times a day, not every two-to-three minutes. They give their full and undivided attention to teachers when they are observing a classroom, not interrupting their focus by constantly checking their social media feed. Most importantly, they set an example for students, who also benefit from focus and whose attention spans are decimated by their own device-driven fragmentation (Newport, 2021).

In coaching leaders for higher degrees of focus, an essential question for every coaching conversation is: "What are your highest priorities right now?" If the answer to that question changes with every coaching session, it's a clue that the client is not engaged in a sufficient level of focus.

EFFECTIVE CLASSROOM INSTRUCTION

By far the most important leading indicator is effective instruction. The elements of effective classroom instruction are not mysterious, despite persistent claims that teaching is more art than science. To be sure, as Robert Marzano (2017) and every veteran teacher I know have argued, there can be an element of artistry to the craft of teaching. These elements are reflected in the spur-of-the-moment decisions to engage a child differently, to notice the otherwise unobserved joys and fears that motivate and demotivate students. But these elements of teaching artistry are not contradictory to the scientific evidence of effective instruction; rather, they are inextricably linked to it. Thus, the art and science of teaching are not contradictory but mutually reinforcing. What both perspectives have in common is that we are engaged in a continuous reflection on what most effectively leads to student success. No matter how elevated the artistry or decisive the external evidence may be, nothing matters unless our practices influence student success.

While classroom instruction is a complex endeavor, many observation protocols have failed to give teachers and administrators the clarity necessary to improve instruction. For example, when Robert Marzano first articulated nine essential instructional strategies, it was not uncommon to see administrators walk into classrooms with the expectation that teachers would miraculously be using all nine of them. These included: the identification of similarities and differences; summarizing and note-taking; reinforcing effort; providing recognition; homework and practice; nonlinguistic representations; setting objectives and providing feedback; generating and testing hypotheses; and questions, cues, and advance organizers. However salutary these ideas may be, the expectation that every lesson and classroom observation include all of these is ludicrous and sends the message to teachers that their evaluation and comments from supervisory observations will be based on a checklist rather than on actual impact on student learning.

When coaching leaders set out to improve classroom instruction, a far better approach is one that is differentiated, based on the needs of each classroom teacher. Some teachers need specific support and feedback on instructional planning, others on feedback and assessment, others on classroom management, others on engagement, and so on. For example, the leader might say, "When I visit your classroom this week, I'm going to focus on student engagement. When you ask a question, I would like to see one hundred percent of students address the question as you give them a minute of think time. In particular, I'd like to see evidence that not only are the students on task but they are also actively learning. This means the teacher calls on them—preferably using equity sticks or other random calling methods—and when they don't know the right answer, I will have the opportunity to see them improve their learning in real time. Perhaps you will use pairs or small groups or other techniques, but to be clear, what I'm looking for is real-time student learning—not just having them recite answers that they already knew before they walked into the classroom."

ACCURATE FEEDBACK FOR STUDENTS

No matter how great the classroom instruction may be, students will not benefit from it if they do not receive accurate feedback on their performance. The best synthesis of the evidence concludes that when feedback is accurate and timely, it is a powerful influence on student achievement (Hattie, 2013). The challenge is that teachers and administrators are drowning in data of widely varying quality and relevance. Enormous amounts of time are wasted in reviewing the scores from the state tests administered the previous year to students who are no longer in the teacher's class.

Although many schools and districts claim to use formative assessments, there is a wide variety of quality in these assessments. Just because an assessment is administered before the end of the year does not necessarily make it formative. When the results are delivered weeks after the student performance, it makes it very difficult for teachers to use those assessments to inform teaching and learning. In addition, many assessments give only the most general information to teachers about student learning needs. Ideally, teachers should not only have student scores, but also the specific test items that students missed. This is especially important in schools where there are significant numbers of English learners. Sometimes a missed item may be due to, for example, deficient math skills. But other times the real root of the error is not math at all, but the English vocabulary in the question.

Finally, if the assessment information is to be used to understand how different teaching practices influence student results, it is imperative that the data are displayed for each separate classroom. This is an enormous psychological barrier in many schools, where any hint of comparing the performance of one teacher to another goes against the culture of social cohesion and the absence of comparison. Teachers have a legitimate fear that comparisons can be used against them. As one teacher explained, data can be "weaponized" in a way that undermines relationships among teachers and administrators. But the fact that data can be used inappropriately is not an argument against the wise use of data; rather, it is an argument in favor of the careful linking of results with professional practices in a way that consistently reveals the most effective teaching practices. This sort of effective analysis is, in sum, a treasure hunt, not a witch hunt.

Teachers uniformly believe that the feedback they provide to students is accurate, but there can be significant inconsistencies in the way that teachers evaluate the same piece of work. The only way to assure accurate feedback to students is a collaborative scoring protocol in which different teachers look at the same piece of student work—perhaps an essay, lab report, or graph in a math or science class. Then each teacher, working alone, evaluates the work, using a scoring guide or rubric. Only after each teacher has completed the evaluation do they reveal their rating to the group. When the ratings are consistent—at least 80% of the teachers come to the same conclusion—then the group can move on to the next piece of student work. But when there are inconsistent evaluations, the next step is not an argument about who is the superior evaluator of student work.

Rather, teachers—all bright and capable college-educated professionals—should scrutinize the scoring rubric for ambiguity. After all, if professional educators can't apply the rubric consistently, it is very unlikely that students can understand the expectations. When inconsistencies occur, this is an opportunity for teachers to improve the clarity and specificity of the rubric.

We've conducted experiments in which teachers repeat a collaborative scoring process four times and two results emerge. First, consistency improves with practice. As the rubric becomes clearer and teachers gain a better understanding of how to apply it, their level of agreement increases. In addition, with practice, teachers score student work at a significantly faster pace. This requires persistence, and when teams of teachers give up on the process of collaborative scoring after only one or two attempts, they never achieve the gains in consistency, accuracy, and speed that come with practice.

The other source of inaccuracy in feedback to students is the widely inconsistent grading practices that prevail in many schools. In theory, students with the same performance on tests, quizzes, and daily assignments—with the same attendance and same behavior—should receive the same grades. But when we have provided the identical student data to more than 10,000 teachers and administrators, we consistently find that the same student work can receive grades ranging from A to F, depending not on variation in the quality of student work but on the idiosyncratic grading policies of the classroom teacher (D. B. Reeves, 2016).

The single best remedy for improving the accuracy of feedback to students through grading is the simple adherence to the principle of evaluating students based on their achievement of academic standards, not on the average of their performance throughout the marking period. Although most electronic grading systems persist in using the average as the basis of calculating student grades, this practice is not only inaccurate—it punishes students at the end of the marking period for mistakes that they made months earlier—but also undermines the very social and emotional skills that schools claim to value. The use of the average tells students, "We don't care how resilient you are, how much you persevere, how much you respond to teacher feedback and improve your performance, because we're going to punish you for all of your prior mistakes. All that stuff we told you about building character with resilience, perseverance, and dedicated work—we really didn't mean it." When the case against the average is stated in those terms, it's indefensible. That leaves us wondering why so many schools cling to grading policies that depend on the toxic and inaccurate use of the average.

The final distortion in providing accurate feedback to students is the inclusion of practice, and particularly homework, as part of the student's grade. Effective practice, as we will discuss in the next section, should be challenging and slightly outside of the student's comfort zone. Yet when practice and homework are part of the student's grade, then students are either filling out papers to demonstrate what they knew before they began the assignment or, thanks to abundant homework help online, they are submitting work completed by others that does not represent the students' actual level of achievement. As one teacher told me, "When I stopped grading homework, we started having honest conversations about what the student knew and did not know. When the homework was part of the grade and the student turned in perfect work, they could not admit what they didn't know and then faced failure and embarrassment later in the semester."

Finally, as the school closures associated with the global pandemic made clear, some students had plenty of support at home, including not only online support but guidance from parents and siblings as well. Other students were left adrift with little or no support. When these students failed because of missing or inadequate homework, the teachers were not grading student proficiency—rather, family socioeconomic status. The evidence on the efficacy of homework is clear, with more than 30 studies concluding that the impact for elementary grades is zero and the impact for secondary grades is negligible. (Neason, 2017)

DELIBERATE PRACTICE FOR STUDENTS AND STAFF

The type of practice that has the greatest impact on learning is deliberate, spaced over time, and focused on retrieval of material that the student has not yet mastered (Boser, 2022). When using retrieval practice techniques, such as student-created flash cards and concept maps, there is immediate feedback. When students make an error—as they surely will if they are challenging themselves to work slightly outside of their comfort zone and master new knowledge and skills—those mistakes are followed by feedback, correction, and the immediate opportunity to apply that feedback, leading to better performance.

Unfortunately, this sort of challenging practice is unpopular with students who much prefer to reread material, highlight sentences, and cram for tests (Agarwal & Bain, 2019). Many homework assignments, especially answering questions to which students already know the answers, are the antithesis of deliberate practice.

LASER-LIKE FOCUS ON ACHIEVEMENT

The time and attention of teachers and school administrators is pulled in many directions, with new curriculum, initiatives, discipline, state testing, union issues, and student and staff health concerns leaving little time for the daily focus on student achievement that is the hallmark of high-achieving schools. While nearly all schools claim to focus on achievement, there are two indicators that reflect the true state of the focus of the school. The first is casual conversations by faculty and leaders—the unscripted and unplanned moments in which conversations could have been on any topic of interest. But in schools that display the laser-like focus I am looking for, these conversations are almost always about student performance. Teachers are not merely talking about formal assessments, and certainly not last year's test scores, but about the day-to-day progress that students make. They notice the gains and frustrations that students face and incessantly focus on how tomorrow can be better. They share their ideas with fellow teachers and are never embarrassed to ask colleagues—including those new to the profession—for their advice and insights.

The second indicator of the laser-like focus on achievement is what I have called the "trophy case effect". The trophy case reflects the culture of the school, and it is often the first thing that visitors notice in the main entrance to a school. There are rows of athletic trophies of course, and schools are justifiably proud of their champions. But when a laser-like focus on achievement is in evidence, I see some unusual things in the trophy cases. For example, one middle school of more than 800 students had individual student learning goals posted on note cards behind the glass of the trophy case. A high school with plenty of championship trophies made room for the scientific papers of students that had been submitted for publication. Another posted student creative and nonfiction essays, while others had student musical compositions and poetry. To be clear, there is nothing wrong with the traditional trophies and extracurricular activities; indeed, my research has demonstrated that students who are involved in those activities have higher grades and attendance than students who are not involved in them (Reeves, 2009). Nevertheless, when academic excellence is visibly honored in the same way that state athletic championships are, it makes a statement to every student who crosses the threshold of the schoolhouse door.

COLLABORATIVE SCORING

Many schools invest enormous amounts of time and resources in teacher collaboration. Sometimes these meetings are organized around the principles of Professional Learning Communities, and at other times the labels are different. The purpose of these collaborative meetings, whatever the nomenclature, is to provide consistency and fairness for all students. While it is becoming increasingly common for teachers within the same grade level and subject to plan units together, and somewhat less frequently, to plan common assessments, the most challenging and rare practice is for teachers to sit together, look at a single piece of student work, and see if they agree on how to evaluate it. Even when scoring guides or rubrics are prescribed by educational systems and publishers, different teachers can apply these documents in substantially different ways, undermining the clarity of their expectations of students.

Collaborative scoring requires a degree of vulnerability that makes many teachers uncomfortable. The reluctance is expressed through rationale like, "If another teacher looks at the work of my students and finds it wanting, doesn't that reflect on my ability as a teacher? I'm not comfortable with everyone else in the room judging my students and, by implication, judging me." Despite this reluctance, there are substantial advantages to collaborative scoring of students' work, provided that it is done in a systematic manner.

First, teachers should all look at copies of the same student's work, and ideally, that student is anonymous. In some schools, teachers ensure anonymity by looking at work from a student in the same grade and subject but from another school, so that no one knows the identity of the student, teacher, or school. Then each teacher, working alone, evaluates the student work, assigning either a grade or a rubric score. Then teachers reveal their scores to one another so that their degree of consistency can be calculated. If four out of five teachers agree that this piece of work is a 3, or perhaps a letter grade of B, then the collaboration score is 80%—four out of five.

But it is not unusual for there to be a wide dispersion in grades as teachers interpret and apply the scoring guides differently. The remedy for these disagreements is not an argument or the assertion that one teacher's standards and expectations are superior to those of her colleagues. Rather, the phrase I use in these discussions is this: the enemy is never one another; the enemy is ambiguity. The remedy is not an argument; rather, it is to identify the flaws in the scoring rubric and correct them, so that the probability of agreement in scoring—and consistent messages to students—is much greater. This takes some time—typically the scoring of four or five different student work samples, with improvements in the scoring rubric after each round. But when teachers persist in a regular program of collaborative scoring, then not only does the fairness and consistency of the messages to students improve but teachers get faster at the entire collaborative process that, while somewhat time-consuming initially, saves teachers enormous amounts of time in scoring essays as well as performance items in math, science, and social studies.

In schools and districts organized as professional learning communities, collaborative scoring is absolutely imperative. The staff cannot answer the first two questions of the PLC—what do we want students to learn and how will we know if they learned it—without collaborative scoring. The failure to engage in this essential process is what Rick DuFour (the preeminent exponent of PLC's) and I called "PLC Lite" (DuFour & Reeves, 2016). The leading indicator that coaches can observe is either direct observation of team meetings or a review of the notes from these meetings to quickly determine the frequency and effectiveness of collaborative scoring.

COMPREHENSIVE NONFICTION WRITING

One of the most powerful leading indicators of student achievement is the commitment of the school to nonfiction writing. Nonfiction writing is strongly associated with gains in achievement, even when every other variable—socioeconomic status, teacher assignment policies, and per pupil funding—is the same. The impact is not just in improved writing, but a pervasive cross-disciplinary impact in math, science, and social studies (Reeves, 2020a). In the best implementation of this leading indicator, nonfiction writing takes place in every grade, kindergarten through twelfth grade, in every subject. We have seen this occur in high-poverty schools that made dramatic progress because every faculty member (including not only English language arts but also math, science, physical education, art, music, social studies, career and technical education)—everyone—engaged in nonfiction writing. To be sure, these schools did not impose complex writing rubrics on math teachers, but they did require that once per month teachers asked students to write and evaluate the writing using a simplified rubric that any teacher in any subject can use.

EXPLICIT INSTRUCTIONAL LEADERSHIP

Principals and other school administrators are expected to be instructional leaders, an expectation that rests on the presumption that those charged with observing and evaluating teachers know what effective instruction is. Sometimes this is true, with the administrators able to state explicit expectations for the instructional practices of teachers from a solid evidence-based perspective (Marshall, 2013). Ideally, they use simple and clear observation forms, such as those listed in the Appendices to this book. These are much simpler and less cumbersome than the observation forms we frequently see used by instructional coaches and school administrators. Moreover, they can be differentiated, as some teachers need more support on instructional planning, others on feedback, others on classroom management, and so forth.

Only when school leaders focus on the leading indicator of teaching practices can they hope to provide sustainable improvements in student performance. Unfortunately, many states remain focused not on the leading indicator, but the lagging indicator—test scores—and while careers and professional futures hang in the balance, they are unable to explain what makes a great teacher great or an ineffective teacher ineffective.

***

We now turn our attention to results indicators, with a focus on attendance, engagement, and achievement. In the more than two decades since the passage of No Child Left Behind in the United States, annual test scores are the coin of the realm for evaluation of districts, schools, administrators, and teachers. Therefore, coaches must pay attention to these indicators. Nevertheless, if the coach focuses exclusively on these indicators, they will provide scant meaningful assistance to the clients they seek to serve.

QUESTIONS FOR REFLECTION:

1. Of the leading indicators you have learned about in this chapter, which ones are most relevant to your role as coach, leader, or teacher? Specifically, how would you apply these indicators to your responsibilities?
2. What are the barriers to using leading indicators in your role?
3. How are classroom observation protocols currently in use in your school or system similar to or different from the exemplary teaching practices discussed in this chapter?

CHAPTER 15

RESULTS INDICATORS

> - ❖ Attendance
> - ❖ Engagement
> - ❖ Achievement
> - ❖ Growth
> - ❖ Personal Results

IN THIS CHAPTER WE CONSIDER THE IMPORTANCE OF RESULTS INDIcators for coaches and clients. In brief, the goals are what the client wishes to achieve—for students, schools, and for the client personally. The leading indicators we considered in the previous chapter are how they will achieve those results. Nearly every reader has been admonished that goals must be SMART, an acronym that varies among publications but in general refers to goals that are Specific, Measurable, Achievable, Relevant, and Time-Bound. In some publications, the R represents "realistic" but that seems to be redundant with achievable. When my colleagues and I analyzed the characteristics of goals in school plans and their relationship to gains in student achievement, we found that the first two elements of SMART goals—specific and measurable—were by far the most important characteristics of effective goals (Reeves, 2013). While attention to results is certainly an important part of the coaching relationship, the coach has a responsibility to focus on the relationship between causes and effects.

As the chart in Figure 15.1 suggests, the relationship between causes and effects can fall into four categories, originally designed as the Leadership and Learning Matrix (Reeves, 2020b). The vertical axis represents the results achieved by the school, district, or client. As you look from the bottom to the top of the matrix, the results improve. Thus, the top half of the chart represents great results, and the bottom half represents low results. But results are not enough. The horizontal axis represents the client's understanding of how those results were achieved. As you read from left to right, the understanding of results improves. Thus, in the upper left-hand quadrant—high results with little understanding of how you achieved those results—is not a reflection of good practice but of luck. We see this in schools when the student population changes due to local boundary changes, leading to an increase in the socioeconomic status of the students, and not surprisingly, the achievement "improves", not due to any actions of teachers or leaders but merely due to factors outside of their control. The converse can occur when achievement decreases, not due to teaching and leadership actions but due to externalities beyond the control of teachers and leaders.

In the lower left-hand quadrant, low results—and little understanding of why the results are low—are unfortunately common in the post-pandemic era. While the semantics of "learning loss" are hotly debated around the nation, the plain fact is that substantial numbers of students whose schools were closed in 2020 and 2021 lost enormous amounts of instruction and learning in reading and math, as well as lost skills in organization, collaboration, and other executive function skills (Goldstein, 2022). Despite the impact of the pandemic-related school closures on student achievement, the vast majority of schools we have observed in 2022 have the same schedule, interventions, and time allocated to student literacy as was the case in 2019. It is as if they are engaging in the magical thinking that the pandemic never happened. This gives rise to a critical coaching question: If you want your results to be different, what are the different decisions in leadership and teaching that you are making to reflect that desired change?

In the Learning quadrant in the lower right-hand corner of the matrix, the results may be low, but the leaders and teachers in the school demonstrate a deep understanding of the causes of low achievement, and they are taking decisive action in time allocation, curriculum, assessment, and teaching practices to address those concerns and improve achievement results. While superficially, the losing and learning quadrants may appear to be the same when merely reporting results, there is a vast difference between the schools that are doomed to repeat their mistakes for lack of understanding of the underlying causes of low achievement and the schools that are on the path to learning and attending to the leading indicators—the essential causes of improved student results. In the upper right-hand quadrant—the Leading schools, leaders, and teachers—there is not only great achievement but also a deep understanding of how they achieved those results. This requires constant vigilance, because a focus only on celebrating great results without understanding how those results were achieved will create an environment in which the school can easily slide from right to left—from Leading to Lucky.

Lucky	Leading
Great results, low understanding of causes	Great results, high understanding of causes
Losing	Learning
Low results, low understanding of causes	Low results, growing understanding of causes

Figure 15.1. The Leadership and Learning Matrix

ATTENDANCE

Certainly, attendance is one of the most important results indicators in any school. When students are not in school, it is unlikely that they are learning. The challenge is how to measure attendance, and statistics such as "average daily attendance" may not reveal actionable information that helps teachers and leaders make better decisions. Typically, a few students account for a disproportionately high level of absences, often missing weeks or months at a time. This is particularly true in very transient communities when students move from one school to another or even to a different country, often without informing the school administration that they are leaving. This leaves a string of "absences" in the school records that may or may not accurately reflect the actual attendance of students. In addition, there are often inconsistencies in how absences are accounted for within a single school district. Some secondary schools, for example, track attendance at the beginning of the school day. If a student is absent from the first-period class, they are counted as absent for the entire day. In other schools, attendance is tracked for each class period, so a student who oversleeps and misses the first period but is present for the remainder of the day receives credit for attendance. This causes chaos when leaders attempt to understand the relationship between leadership practices designed to encourage attendance and the data on attendance results. If the results are not calculated in a consistent way, the inferences that district leaders made about leadership decision-making are worthless.

Finally, it is important to note the role that teachers and leaders play in influencing student attendance. Although it is tempting to accept with resignation that attendance is just one of those factors wholly influenced by home environment, we have consistently seen examples where the diligent efforts of teachers and leaders have, with identical home environments, led to dramatic improvements in attendance.

In addition to general measurements such as "average daily attendance", coaches should help clients look at attendance data in different ways. Examples include:

- Percentage of students with 90% or greater attendance: This is particularly helpful when analyzing student failure data. While student failures are often attributed to poor attendance, a focus on students who attend school 90% or more of the time shifts the focus of student failure from students and their families to what is happening inside the school.

- Percentage of students who are chronically absent: Chronic absenteeism may be defined as 20 or more absences, and although this is typically a very small number of students, they can distort attendance data because they account for a large number of absences.
- Percentage of students present for 80% of the school day: This data point avoids the distortions that occur in which a doctor's appointment, family obligation, or late arrival might otherwise be counted as an absence for the full day.

ENGAGEMENT

Because engagement can mean different things to different people, it is important to define terms. Douglas Fisher, Nancy Frey, and I have suggested that by engagement, we mean the mutually focused attention of students and teachers on curiosity, challenge, and learning. This definition implies that however entertaining a lecture might be when delivered as a soliloquy by a talented teacher in a classroom or an administrator in a staff meeting, those presentations may be called entertainment, but they cannot be called engagement.

ACHIEVEMENT

The most common way that student achievement results are measured is through annual testing. These numbers grab the headlines in the media and are often significant influences on teacher and administrator evaluation. The central problem with using annual state test scores as results indicators, however, is that by the time teachers and leaders receive this information, it is too late to respond to the data in any meaningful way. There are better ways to measure student achievement in a way that can, as the previous chapter suggests, lead to a meaningful relationship between causes (leading indicators) and effects (results indicators). These include:

- Percentage of students reading at or above grade level: It is imperative that reading levels are calibrated in a way that all teachers agree on the accuracy of the result. Running Records, for example, can be an excellent way for teachers to assess reading levels, but only if teachers are scrupulous in how they assess student performance. It is helpful if, for example, teachers view a video of a student reading and, before the teacher leading the assessment reveals his conclusion, the teachers watching the video share their assessments. There are also many automated reading assessments that yield consistent scoring but do not allow the teachers to have complete understanding of the items that the student marked correctly and incorrectly.
- Percentage of students writing at a proficient or higher level in nonfiction writing assignments: The evidence is clear that this particular indicator is strongly associated with better student performance in reading comprehension, math, science, and social studies. Our work in schools where writing is consistently required in every subject and every grade demonstrates that this single professional practice is strongly predictive of student success. As with reading comprehension, the key to accurate assessment of writing performance is an agreement by the faculty of what the word "proficient" means. The only way to assure this is the consistent practice of collaborative scoring.
- Percentage of D/F Rate: This is especially important in secondary schools, and the evidence is clear that reducing this particular indicator is strongly associated with better behavior, attendance, and classroom climate and culture.

It is important not to be overwhelmed with too many achievement indicators. Some assessment systems provide so many reports, charts, and graphs that teachers and leaders are overwhelmed.

GROWTH

The Every Student Succeeds Act (ESSA) explicitly endorses growth measures for accountability for student achievement (DuFour, et. al., 2017). The best way to measure growth is by comparing the performance of the same students to themselves. That is, Javier and Janet's scores are not compared to those of their predecessors in last year's group of students but to their own scores in previous weeks and months. The question is not how did this year's class compare to last year's class? Rather it is, to what extent are the students I have right now improving compared to when they started my class?

We have seen both quantitative and qualitative ways in which teachers demonstrate growth. In quantitative teams, they can show the percentage of students who were proficient in essential skills as the year progresses. In order to demonstrate growth, it is imperative that teachers are honest with students at the beginning of the school year. For many students and parents who are always expecting perfect scores, it may come as a shock that students are not proficient at the beginning of the school year. We have found it helps to remind these parents, who depend upon perfect scores by their children, that the reason their children come to school is that they are not proficient in everything. Any assessment that reveals that these students are not yet meeting standards is not a mark of shame but an indicator that there is work to be done by every student, and that is why they should come to school every day.

PERSONAL RESULTS

The key to achieving organizational goals, the coach will soon discover, is the degree to which the client can recall and articulate their personal success in setting and achieving goals. Perhaps it was a change in setting, an incremental "one day at a time" technique, or mindfully considering their actions before taking a hit of sugar, tobacco, or alcohol (Fogg, 2021). Perhaps it was a friend or mentor to whom they made a commitment for regular exercise. Perhaps it was a major goal, such as finishing a doctoral dissertation, running a marathon, or a commitment to fully engaged family time without work or technology interruptions for a full day every week. The ability of a client to set and achieve a personal goal will provide essential insights for the client and coach as they approach challenging goals at work.

Some clients achieved their personal goals entirely on their own, working independently. Others needed external support, such as a family member, physician, trainer, or coach to help them achieve their goals. Some clients will reveal that they tracked their personal goal-achieving every day, something I have done for decades. I share this personal detail not because it always leads to achievement of my goals—I consistently get about half of them done every year—but because it shows my coach how I think and work. I like to keep score and to be accountable, and this motivates me to do better, whether it is maintaining my health, focusing my time, or writing books and articles. In contrast to my compulsive score-keeping, coaches will find clients who have simply developed effective habits without conspicuous goal-setting and tracking. The key is not for the coach to advocate for a particular method; it is for the coach to understand what makes the client succeed in personal goals and then build on those successful techniques for the client's professional goals. While this might seem obvious, there are many instances in which the transfer of personal success to professional success does not take place without supportive coaching. Consider the planning, organization, and discipline required for a successful family vacation in contrast to the chaos that the same person faces at work. While they would never go to Disney World without a plan, schedule, and prioritized goals, their work life might lack all of these characteristics. The coach is not there to tell the client what to do but to persistently inquire what makes the client successful in some areas, such as planning a family vacation—and unsuccessful in other areas, such as leading a staff meeting.

* * *

In this chapter we considered what many people regard as the bottom line of the coaching relationship: results. However, the most effective coaching relationships depend upon a balance of leading indicators with results indicators. In addition, we reflected on the relationship between personal goal achievement by the client and professional goal-setting. Because Fearless Coaching is a strength-based approach, it is essential for the coach to understand where the client has been successful in linking causes and effects in their personal lives and then apply these strengths to a professional setting. In the next chapter we consider the special case of coaching in a crisis.

QUESTIONS FOR REFLECTION:

1. What is the results indicator that is most important for your role as coach, teacher, or leader?
2. Which results indicators receive the greatest attention from your district leadership, governing board, and community?
3. Review the Leadership and Learning Matrix and identify the quadrant that best describes your school and/or district: Lucky, Losing, Learning, or Leading. Why did you come to that conclusion?

CHAPTER 16

COACHING IN A CRISIS

> ❖ Lessons of the Pandemic   ❖ Teacher Shortage
> ❖ School Violence   ❖ Funding Cliffs

WHILE THE GLOBAL PANDEMIC OF 2020–2022 IS THE MOST RECENT crisis that most readers recall, it is certainly not the only crisis that educators and school leaders have faced. As this book goes to press, Ukrainian refugees are pouring into Poland, and some schools are seeing their student population expand dramatically with traumatized students who have been displaced, have witnessed the ravages of war, and do not speak the language of the Polish classroom. Students on every continent have faced similar challenges of language, displacement, and trauma, while teachers and administrators are expected to pick up the pieces. Schools in the United States have received tens of thousands of students from Afghanistan who are only the most recent wave of young refugees to find a welcome home in American schools.

Readers who joined our profession before 2001 will recall the trauma of the 9/11 terrorist attacks which affected students not only in New York and Washington but around the world as students and staff members wondered when the next attack would come. Just a few years later, the great recession of 2008–2010 struck, displacing students and families from their homes and creating unemployment, home foreclosures, and economic uncertainties that affected students and families for years. In this chapter we consider the lessons of the global pandemic and how it affected students and teachers; school violence and the dramatic increase in gun access and shootings; the pervasive shortage of teachers and substitutes; and the predictable funding cliffs that will affect the budgets of nearly every school system.

LESSONS OF THE PANDEMIC

When Chinese Premier Chou En-lai was asked by U.S. Secretary of State Henry Kissinger about the impact of the French Revolution, which began in 1789, the Chinese leader replied, "It is too soon to tell." When one's view of history extends to millennia rather than months, the long-term view may come naturally. Nevertheless, it is not too early to draw at least some lessons from the recent pandemic that will inform other crises that coaches and their clients must face. Here are five preliminary lessons learned that are relevant to coaches, leaders, and institutions as a result of the pandemic:

1. Leaders must maintain a bias for action. When a crisis, especially one with lethal consequences, is ongoing, people need action. Researchers will debate for years the extent to which masks and handwashing were effective during the pandemic, but leaders who took decisive action to use the best available science to maintain the health of their colleagues and communities were wise to do so.
2. Assess risks clearly and publicly. During the pandemic, most people focused only on the risk of the disease, and that is what led to pervasive school closures. But there are other risks to consider as well, including: the risks of food insecurity for students whose primary source of food was the meals provided in school; physical safety, especially for students who were demonstrably safer at school than when left alone in housing

projects; and emotional safety, particularly for students whose strongest and most consistent relationships were with classroom teachers. Leaders have an obligation to make clear that there are no risk-free leadership decisions and policies. Rather, they must choose among different risks. When we consider the pervasive learning loss associated with school closures, the increase in child abuse, and the physical and emotional effects of students left alone at home, leaders will reconsider the wisdom of the immediate reaction to close schools. Coaches have the obligation to ask, in the face of difficult decisions, what the risks are of all decision alternatives, a process too seldom used during the pandemic.

3. Monitor short-term indicators and make mid-course corrections. Many of the promises of online learning turned out to be illusions. While schools did a fairly good job, except in remote and rural areas, of delivering technology and connectivity, they failed to assess the degree to which students actually used technology to improve learning. In some schools, students were online for only an hour per day, and the expectation was that students would make use of the rest of the day for asynchronous learning—doing homework and seeking teacher assistance where necessary. This was a pipe dream, and the failure of the promise of distance learning was quickly apparent in the early days of school closures. Nevertheless, once employees had become accustomed to working from home for only a few hours a day, it became very difficult to expect them to return to work. Organizations representing employees asserted that educational leaders had to guarantee a safe environment before employees and students should return to school, and this created the utterly false and unsupportable expectation that there was any such thing as a guaranteed safe environment.

4. Heroism is not a sustainable strategy. For every teacher who enjoyed the one-hour-a-day work life, there were many teachers who labored for 18 hours a day, answering calls and texts

from students and parents, day and night. While the sacrificial labors of these teachers were undeniably heroic, no system can depend upon these exceptional efforts as a strategy. Indeed, teacher burnout is a primary reason that the turnover in the teaching profession soared during and after the pandemic (Brantlinger, 2021).

5. Money doesn't buy a 25-hour day. While schools in the U.S. were showered with additional funding during school closures associated with the pandemic, the proliferation of programs did not gain teachers the one asset that unlimited funding cannot buy: time. Effective coaches were continually required to help clients focus on the essentials, rather than respond positively to every new opportunity that additional funds provided.

SCHOOL VIOLENCE

Each year, an estimated 26 million students in the U.S. are victims of school violence, with girls and young women as well as gender nonconforming youth at particular risk (Gupta, 2022). The impact of this physical and psychological violence is not only on the direct victims of violence, but also on those who observe the violence. Among the many risk factors for identifying those students likely to commit violent acts against other students is poor academic performance. This suggests a very counterintuitive strategy for educators and leaders. When faced with the threat of violence, the impulse of staff members may be, "First we have to put the hammer down and get this place under control, and then we'll worry about academic achievement." But the evidence suggests that a key strategy in reducing school violence is to reduce the student failure rate and the hopelessness and despair that accompanies it.

TEACHER SHORTAGE

Before the global pandemic began, the turnover of teachers was approximately 8% per year. As schools reopen after the pandemic, the percentage of teachers leaving the profession has expanded to 20%, two-and-a-half times greater than the previous two years, and this number threatens to grow (U.S. Department of Education, 2022). The challenge facing educational leaders today is to retain the best teachers currently serving schools and also to reinvigorate the pipeline, with high-school and college students finding that teaching is an honorable and rewarding profession. While, certainly, money is a part of the solution—you can't manage six-figure debt with a five-figure income—money alone is not sufficient to retain teachers. Other leadership factors, including respect, professional autonomy, collaboration, and professional learning are keys to retaining and attracting teachers (Reeves, 2018).

FUNDING CLIFFS

School systems throughout the U.S. face a severe funding shortage that is caused by two factors. First, the federal funds associated with COVID relief will expire in the 2023–2024 school year. Schools that used money for recurring expenses, such as teacher raises, will find that they can no longer afford to fund these raises, and that will require either reductions in teacher salaries (very unlikely) or a dramatic increase in class sizes and reductions in other budget items. Second, the primary variable in state funding for school systems is the student population, and many students have simply not returned to school even as schools reopened after the pandemic (Mitropoulos, 2021).

* * *

In this chapter we considered the special case of coaching teachers and leaders in times of crisis. While the global pandemic may be the defining crisis for the careers of many educators and leaders now in the education profession, the likelihood of additional crises to come—recession, war, and political upheaval—is great. Fortunately, we can be informed by the crises of the past and be better prepared to deal with them. In the next chapter we consider how to put all the lessons learned in this book together in order to make Fearless Coaching a success for every stakeholder.

QUESTIONS FOR REFLECTION:

1. What were your greatest lessons learned during the global pandemic of 2020–2022?
2. If you had one decision during the pandemic to reconsider and change, what would it be?
3. How can you help new educators and leaders who are joining the profession after the pandemic learn from your experiences?

CHAPTER 17

PUTTING IT ALL TOGETHER: FROM COACHING TO THE CLASSROOM

- ❖ Finding the Islands of Excellence
- ❖ Meaningful Celebrations
- ❖ Replication: Expanding the Client's Impact
- ❖ Do Now: Creating a Sense of Urgency
- ❖ Coaching Coaches

WE NOW COME TO THE END OF OUR JOURNEY INTO THE PRACTICE OF Fearless Coaching. While coaching can be a very rewarding experience for both coach and client, there are inevitable frustrations along the way. Therefore, we begin this chapter with a relentless search for success even in the most challenging of circumstances. These are the islands of excellence, surrounded by troubled waters. When coaches celebrate with a client, it is deliberate, meaningful, and based on real growth and achievement. One of the greatest challenges for the coach is helping clients expand their influence. In the parlance of the

Leadership Performance Matrix (Reeves, 2008),[2] the Level 3 leader has an impact on that leader's school, but the Level 4 leader has an impact on the entire system. That is the greatest leverage in a coaching relationship. Complacency is the enemy of progress, and therefore coaches must continually create a sense of urgency for the next actions with every client. Every coaching conversation must end with a commitment to next steps—what the client will do immediately in order to take the work to the next level of performance. Finally, we consider how coaches can support other coaches and expand the influence of a coaching culture through the entire system.

FINDING THE ISLANDS OF EXCELLENCE

Coaches are frequently engaged to solve problems, and it is therefore tempting to have coaching conversations focus on the toughest issues confronting the client. While that is a reasonable investment of time and energy for the coach, the best source for addressing those challenges is not the wisdom and experience of the coach; rather, it is the islands of excellence that are right in front of the client if only the client could focus on successes rather than failures. These islands of excellence are all around us. It is the exceptional class of eager and excited readers in a school that, to look at the test scores of the school or those of the district, one would conclude is a literary desert. It is the enthusiastic leader who finds something to celebrate in every student and staff member, despite the relentless drumbeat of threats from higher headquarters. It is the school that is a beacon of hope in a blighted neighborhood, because the staff knows not only every student, but every parent, and makes the school the most welcoming and safe institution in the entire community.

In almost every instance in which a client has raised a seemingly intractable problem, the question the skillful coach asks is: "Where

---

[2] Free download at: https://static1.squarespace.com/static/56a6ae1c22482e2f99869834/t/6012d0317f0da2016a9e2c0e/1611845682131/Reeves+Leadership+Performance+Matrix.pdf

is this working well for you?" Reading scores are low: "Where are they great, even if only in a single classroom or a group within a classroom?" Teacher morale is low: "Do you have an example of a supremely engaged and committed classroom educator?" Client focus and energy are low: Discover the last time the client felt in a state of flow, fully engaged and operating with a sense of optimism and purpose. It might have been outside of the professional environment and perhaps in the distant past, but almost every client can recall such a state, and these memories are the keys to unlocking motivation for the present and future.

The islands of excellence are there for every client, perhaps in the room down the hall or in memories of times past. But the islands are there, and the job of the coach is to find those islands, make those images as vivid as possible, and then replicate them for the future.

MEANINGFUL CELEBRATIONS

Tom Peters, (Peters & Carr, 2013; Peterson & Johnson, 2017) perhaps one of the most influential leadership consultants in the past half century, tells the story of the time a leader observed great performance and wanted to celebrate the success immediately. The leader reached into a fruit bowl and pulled out a banana and presented it to the astonished recipient. That started a tradition of "the golden banana" award that was presented for outstanding performance. It was not a big bonus, promotion, or trophy—just a banana—but it represented an authentic celebration of exceptional performance in real time. Coaches should also provide celebratory moments, but they must be authentic and timely. While bananas are not necessarily required, coaches can provide celebration of client success in the form of letters to the client's supervisor, articles in professional publications, and personal notes of encouragement and appreciation.

Celebrations need not be expansive or public. Some people prefer to have a private moment of affirmation rather than a round of applause. Coaches are in an especially good position to say, "I'm so proud of you," and "I know that this victory was particularly hard-won." Because the coach has been privy to many experiences of disappointment and failure that the client has faced, the celebration of success by the coach can be especially meaningful and authentic.

REPLICATION: EXPANDING THE CLIENT'S IMPACT

In order for the coach to have maximum impact and serve the client organization, it is vital that the work of each individual coaching client is replicated. For example, a common way in which coaches support clients is through improving the accuracy and specificity of feedback. This is especially impactful because we know that, just as effective feedback for students is a significant driver of student achievement, effective feedback for adults is a substantial driver of teaching and leadership effectiveness. It is therefore essential that when the client learns how to provide fair, accurate, specific, and timely feedback, this skill is transmitted throughout the client's realm of influence. The coaching provided, for example, to a single principal on effective feedback, can influence 100 teachers and, in turn, influence thousands of students.

Consider also the impact of effective time management from a single client to an entire school or system. Just as organizational drag—unnecessary meetings, ineffective use of time, duplicative and unnecessary systems—can weigh down an entire system due to the lethargy and inefficiency of a single leader (Mankins & Garton, 2017), so also can a single incremental improvement in effective meetings, task organization, and project management create time and energy for an entire school and system. An especially helpful coaching question is, "Since our last meeting, with whom have you shared your insights and ideas?"

DO NOW: CREATING A SENSE OF URGENCY

Harvard Business School Professor John Kotter is among the world's foremost experts on change. Yet I have noticed that many self-proclaimed change leaders are fonder of quoting Kotter's work from the 1980s than his more reflective work of the 21st century in which he noted that the vast majority of organizational change efforts fail. Kotter has analyzed these failures and, with breathtaking honesty and reflection, concludes that one of the most significant reasons for the failure of change is the failure to create a sufficient sense of urgency. In the classrooms of particularly effective teachers, the words *Do Now* appear on the board as students file into their seats. These are the teachers who make use of every second of class time, knowing that time is precious and evaporating. While they have the same number of minutes as every one of their colleagues, these teachers make every moment count, starting with the Do Now requirements that begin the moment the students walk into the room. Coaches and clients should learn from the examples of great teachers with Do Now commitments.

What are the items that are so urgent and important that they are not consigned to a to-do list but are undertaken immediately? Urgency is both short-term and long-term. The coach can best support the client by asking long-term questions. What are the challenges that we will face decades from now if we do not address them today? For example, there are clear predictors of high-school dropouts that start in elementary school: literacy, attendance, retention, and interpersonal skills. If those issues are not addressed, then dropouts are inevitable. When a student fails to complete high school, it is not merely a failure for this year but for the next 40 years, during which that dropout will suffer persistent poverty, unemployment, medical care needs, and excessive involvement in the criminal justice system. When clients act with a sense of urgency, they not only address short-term goals, but also address long-term failures that will serve their stakeholders well.

There are also short-term client needs to consider. In order to find the source of a sense of urgency for the client, coaches should ask,

"What is keeping you awake at night?" If coaches are to maximize their support for clients, and the clients are to maximize their impact on the school or system they are serving, then this is the essential question that must be addressed. While clients may be concerned about academic achievement and attendance, but what is keeping them awake at night is an interpersonal issue with their administrative assistant or a conflict with their supervisor, then the coach is ill-advised to get into the weeds of strategic plans and goals without addressing the central challenge that the client is facing.

COACHING COACHES

Coaches who are supporting senior leaders will often come to the point that the client wishes to build a coaching organization. This places the client in the position of eventually coaching other coaches in order to establish a coaching culture throughout the organization. While the subject of coaching coaches is the focus of another book, let us briefly address the importance of coaching coaches now.

In order to develop a coaching culture, it is imperative that senior leaders distinguish the role of coaches from other roles, especially from the role of evaluator. If the client is to be prepared to be a coach for other coaches, then the client must first have successfully fulfilled the role of client and demonstrate an understanding of what effective coaching is from the client's point of view. The coaching of other coaches is particularly challenging when the coaches are dealing with confidential information. The coach owes the client, with the few exceptions that were noted in Chapter 4, absolute confidentiality. Therefore, those coaching the coaches must have a high degree of trust in the coaches and their clients throughout the system. While the coach of coaches can ask about trends in goal-setting and persistent themes in client challenges, the coach of coaches cannot ask, "What are the problems that James is facing?" or "Why do you think Julie is struggling?" The coach is not the intermediary between the client and senior leadership; rather, the coach is there to build capacity among the clients so that they can address these issues directly with their supervisors.

***

QUESTIONS FOR REFLECTION:

1. Think about a school or classroom facing particularly great challenges. Where are their islands of excellence? Try to describe those islands in vivid detail so that you can attempt to replicate their success.
2. What celebration can you plan now? It might be for a group or just for a single person. But don't go to the next section without some specific affirmation that you can offer to a client or colleague.
3. What is a Do Now for you? Something that is of such great urgency that it will be the next thing that you do regardless of other priorities on your task list?
4. What will be required to expand the impact of coaching throughout the school or district you are serving? How can you build a culture of coaching coaches?

AFTERWORD

FEARLESS COACHING AND THE GREATER GOOD— FOUR CROSSROADS FOR EVERY COACHING RELATIONSHIP

- ❖ Persistence through Adversity
- ❖ Raising the Bar
- ❖ Leveraging Impact through Others
- ❖ Relentless Focus

THIS BOOK HAS MADE THE CASE THAT FEARLESS COACHING CAN have a profoundly positive impact on the client and the client's organization. Nevertheless, in every coaching relationship there will be decision points at which both coach and client must decide how to improve the effectiveness of the coaching relationship and whether to continue it. The ultimate criterion for these decision points is the degree to which the coaching relationship supports the greater good.

PERSISTENCE THROUGH ADVERSITY

The first crossroad is the willingness of the client and coach to persevere through adversity. Whether the adversity is a pervasive and existential threat, such as the global pandemic—or the daily trials of schools, such as toxic political influence, personal criticisms, or disappointments in performance—each situation must be faced with either persistence or passivity. The latter approach is tempting. After all, the coach may reason, my client is hurting and exhausted, everyone is burned out, and now is not the time to challenge them any further. This passive approach, however tempting, is most likely to lead to the perpetuation of the very conditions that afflicted the client and school. For example, during the school shutdowns associated with the pandemic, some schools suspended professional learning and anything resembling accountability for schools. Administrators stopped observing classrooms, teachers stopped expecting anything but the minimum engagement of students. District leaders stopped taking seriously requirements for attendance and student results. "We're just trying to survive here," was the common refrain.

In other schools and districts, by contrast, teachers and leaders persisted through the pain. With exceptional efforts by staff members, attendance that had been languishing at 50% rose to pre-pandemic levels. Student engagement, which had been nearly nonexistent with cameras turned off and little or no work submitted, was transformed into clear and consistent evidence of learning. Professional learning, even in times when teachers were stressed to the maximum degree possible, continued because leaders knew that collaboration and professional learning were antidotes to stress, not causes of it.

During World War II, the British motto was Keep Calm and Carry On, even as relentless bombing campaigns by the Nazis disrupted daily life. For those educational systems that maintained coaching as a vital source of intellectual, emotional, and organizational nourishment during the global pandemic, this calm and deliberate persistence was a key factor in their survival and success. By their example, these teachers and leaders not only met their own needs but served as examples for their communities and the nation.

RAISING THE BAR

The second crossroad coaches and clients must face is complacency, and the extent to which they are willing to raise the bar. At Creative Leadership Solutions, we have the "five-minute rule" which states that if you make a colossal blunder, you are permitted to fret about it for 4 minutes and 59 seconds, and then get back to work. When you do something spectacularly well, you are permitted to strut around like a peacock for 4 minutes and 59 seconds, and then get back to work. When clients reach their challenging goals, celebration is certainly appropriate. But soon thereafter, the coach and client must collaborate to raise the bar and continue progress. It is a never-ending pursuit. This shows to every staff member and all the stakeholders who are watching a successful performer that resting on their laurels is never an option. Rather, there is an ethic of continuous progress and relentless pursuit of excellence.

LEVERAGING IMPACT THROUGH OTHERS

The third crossroads is the willingness of the client to leverage impact through others. While the coach-client relationship is an intensely personal one, the coach has an obligation to support not only a single client but also the entire organization. However successful the client may be, if the success of the organization depends on a single person, then the coach has failed. The ultimate responsibility of both coach and client is to build capacity so that continued success depends on neither the client nor the coach, but on the skills that have been built and instilled throughout the organization.

RELENTLESS FOCUS

The fourth crossroad for the coaching relationship is the degree to which the coach will maintain a focus on what matters most. Once a client has achieved success, it is easy for boredom to set in. "We did that last year," the client might claim. "We've already done data analysis, let's move on to something new." This is the logic of the athlete or musician who, having won a competition, stops practicing. While new and greater challenges always lie ahead, the coach does not serve the client well by failing to focus on the essentials and serving as a screen to stop the client from being overwhelmed by the fragmentation associated with initiative fatigue.

What's next? To implement the ideas in this book, we have provided Appendices, each of which can be copied and shared with colleagues. You can also download these at: https://www.creativeleadership.net/fearless-books. My colleagues and I welcome a continued dialogue with readers, and we welcome your success stories as well as your challenges and comments. You can contact the author directly at Douglas.Reeves@CreativeLeadership.net.

APPENDICES: CHECKLISTS FOR COACHES AND CLIENTS

A. Coaching Readiness Checklist: Before the First Call
B. First-Meeting Checklist: Building the Relationship
C. Coaching Conversations about Root Causes
D. Goals Checklist
E. Effective Time Management Checklist
F. Leading Collaborative Teams of Teachers and Administrators Checklist
G. Leading Indicators Checklist
H. Classroom Observation Checklist

APPENDIX A.
COACHING READINESS CHECKLIST:
BEFORE THE FIRST CALL

Before commencement of a coaching relationship, take time to get to know the client and discuss the coaching process. The conversation should be informal and reassuring. It is essential that the coach make clear that the coaching relationship is supportive and nonevaluative, and that the client will be the one setting goals and driving the discussions. The following items can guide the conversation.

Readiness:

- ☐ Client is open to receiving support.
- ☐ Client is motivated to change and learn.
- ☐ Client is ready for a collaborative partnership to learn and achieve results.
- ☐ Client is receptive to one-on-one help and guidance.
- ☐ Client is emotionally healthy and able to give intellectual and psychological energy to the coaching process.
- ☐ Client is willing to commit to a period of significant time and work to make the coaching successful.
- ☐ Client has identified draft goals from which to begin the coaching process.
- ☐ Other Readiness Notes:

Potential Objectives:

- ☐ Decision making
- ☐ Problem solving
- ☐ Skill development
- ☐ Habit change
- ☐ Develop/improve relationships
- ☐ Strategy planning

- ☐ Preparation for a new role (for first- or second-year clients in their current positions)
- ☐ Improving the client's communication with staff and stakeholders
- ☐ Manage change
- ☐ Professional development of the client
- ☐ Conflict resolution
- ☐ Facilitating meetings
- ☐ Leading Professional Learning Communities
- ☐ Time management
- ☐ Other

What is the most important thing the client should accomplish through coaching?

Indicators of Success Criteria:

- ☐ School achievement data
- ☐ School growth data
- ☐ Survey results
- ☐ Other

Contextual Issue(s) That May Impact Success:

- ☐ Union issues
- ☐ Board/District Office
- ☐ Initiatives (list all that may impact)
- ☐ Parent/student demographics
- ☐ Other

Provision of High-Quality Feedback:

- ☐ Understand what effective feedback entails
- ☐ Determine modalities of feedback
- ☐ Structure feedback with/among peers
- ☐ Other

APPENDIX B.
FIRST-MEETING CHECKLIST:
BUILDING THE RELATIONSHIP

In order to best serve the individual to be coached, it is absolutely essential to take time to understand the client. In essence, what drives them? What are their goals? What will the framework of coaching sessions look like (e.g., schedule, etc.)?

This instrument is intended to simplify this process for the coach while guiding the first meeting.

Coach:_____Client: _____

Meeting frequency/duration (identify days/times): _____

1. Tell me a bit about yourself, both personally and professionally.	
2. What would you say drives you? What excites you in your role?	

3. Identify three to five goals you'd like to achieve this year professionally. How do you see me supporting you through this process?	
4. What are five non-negotiables for you? In other words, what are professional attributes you hold absolutely sacred in your practice?	
5. Identify three to five potential roadblocks to your success this year relevant to the goals you've identified.	
6. Explain the criteria you'll want to use to measure success relevant to the goals you've identified. How will these be measured?	

The coach should spend the time to understand client's responses clearly. In many instances, it is recommended the coach take the time to ask the client to "Tell me more about____" as a means of seeking clarity and meaning. During this first meeting, the coach should be taking notes, listening intently, and then summarizing what was heard after each response.

The last step in the process should be to complete the summary below where the coach identifies their own notes regarding what they perceive as potential challenges, goals, etc., as a means to more effectively serve their client.

Coach Summary:

APPENDIX C.
COACHING CONVERSATIONS
ABOUT ROOT CAUSES

Questions to Get to the "Root of the Root":

- When you think about the type of learning you want your students to be doing, what is getting in the way?
- When you think about the type of teaching you want to do, what are some obstacles you're facing? Can you describe that further?
- What can you tell me about that student?
- What have you already tried? What does this look like now in your classroom, and how might it look after it's implemented? How will your classroom look different if the problem is solved? How will student learning be impacted by achieving this goal?
- How might student learning look different if this problem is addressed? What concerns you about _____? What evidence do you have that supports your concerns?
- How might implementing this idea impact _____ (student engagement, student behavior, student collaboration)? Of these different areas of concern, which one might be a good one to focus on first?
- What are some strengths your students are bringing to the table? When you think about where your students are now and where you want them to be, what are some areas where they may need to grow?
- When you think about implementing _____, what might get in the way of success for you and your students? What are some resources that you're already using? Why is this goal important to you?
- How does this area you're wanting to work on tie into areas your school is focused on improving? How might this tie into

an area that your PLC group has identified as a growth area? Tell me more about how you identified this as a goal.
- Are you noticing any patterns when you're observing this behavior? What steps have you previously taken to build a relationship with this person? When was there a time in which you worked well with this person?
- So, what I'm hearing is that you don't feel like you have enough time. What "time" are we referring to—instructional, planning, collaborating?
- What further learning should we do before drafting a plan of action? Who in the school or district might be a good resource for developing a plan?
- What date might be a good time to meet again to share what we've discovered? How might we collect some baseline evidence that would help us measure our progress?

APPENDIX D.
GOALS CHECKLIST

Organizational Goals for Grade-Level Teams, Departments, Schools, and Districts:

1. The goal is SMART (Specific, Measurable, Achievable, Relevant, Time-Bound).
   - ☐ The goal is *specific*; exactly what we will accomplish is clear.
   - ☐ The goal is *measurable*; we will know when we have achieved the goal and what progress we are making along the way.
   - ☐ The goal is *achievable*; we have the resources and time we need to accomplish this goal.
   - ☐ The goal is *relevant*; it directly affects our mission.
   - ☐ The goal is *time-bound*; we know exactly what day the goal will be accomplished.

2. Calendar Commitments:
   - ☐ In order to have the time to achieve the goal, we have specific dates and times on the calendar to allocate to this goal and nothing else.

3. Anticipate Initiative Fatigue:
   - ☐ If we need to cancel other meetings or initiatives in order to achieve this goal, we have done so.

4. Authority:
   - ☐ We have permission from necessary administrative and policy authorities to have the resources and time to achieve the goal. If agreement from collective bargaining units is required to achieve the goal, we have those agreements secured.

5. Alignment:
   - ☐ The goal is consistent with our mission, values, improvement plans, strategic plans, and other documents that direct the work of our organization.

Personal Goals for the Client:

At the onset of the coaching relationship, the client will identify an important goal that will become the focus of every coaching conversation between coach and client. Without a goal to guide the conversation, coaching will lack focus, and learning and growth for the client will be limited, as will be the level of change the client is working to create within the organization. Sometimes a client's goal will emerge during the relationship-building conversation as the client and coach discuss the client's values, hopes, and aspirations. Other times, a client may be feeling overwhelmed and need to rely on the coach to assist in the client's search for clarity in determining a goal. The following questions can assist in this process.

- Is there a district initiative the client is responsible for implementing that is new to the school?
- What goal will have the greatest impact on student achievement?
- What is the client passionate about, so that fulfilling this goal will bring tremendous satisfaction?
- What has the client always wanted to address but has been hesitant to address in the past?
- Is this a measurable goal? How will the client know the goal has been achieved? What will success look like?
- What time frame is the client looking at? Is this a short-term or long-term goal? If it is a long-term goal, what short-term wins can the client look to?
- Are there leadership skills the client wants to strengthen (e.g., giving feedback, communication, having difficult conversations)?

- What new learning is calling the client?
- Will this goal align with the school's overall goals? District goals?
- What are the district's expectations regarding the client's coaching goals?
- Where would the client most like to make a difference?
- Why is that goal important to the client?
- What is currently on the client's plate that is bringing about feelings of anxiety or worry?
- What important process or practice has been successfully implemented in the client's organization but is lacking attention?
- How does the goal align with client's core values?
- What goal, if accomplished, would make the client feel excited, proud, joyful?

A coach recognizes a client's personal life is never truly left at home. Concerns and celebrations regarding family, health, dreams, plans, and challenges impact who the client is when walking through the door at work and will determine the level of energy and attention the client will have available to focus on professional goals. For coaching to have the greatest impact on a client's growth and learning, it is imperative for the coach to be aware of a client's personal/life goals in addition to job-performance goals. Examples are listed here:

- Client is addressing balancing work and home responsibilities.
- Client has moved away from exercise routine (jogging, yoga, gym, home workout), and it is resulting in stress-related issues. Client wants to correct this.
- Client is caring for an elderly parent.
- Client is new to the job and working to overcome limiting beliefs.
- Client is caring for child or spouse with serious health issues.
- Client is trying to establish a reasonable time for leaving work and sticking to it.
- Client is planning a son's or daughter's wedding.
- Client is working on increasing time for self-care.

APPENDIX E.
EFFECTIVE TIME MANAGEMENT CHECKLIST

The essentials of time management are simple, but neither simplistic nor easy.

1. Create a daily prioritized task list (DTPL):

    This is the key to effective time management. A "task" is something that can be accomplished in 45 minutes or less. If 45 minutes is an impossible block of time for you, then you wish to define a "task" as something that can be done in whatever block of time works for you—perhaps 10 or 15 minutes. The DTPL is updated daily. An easy way to do this is with a simple spreadsheet or Trello board, so that the priorities (A, B, C or 1, 2, 3) can be automatedly sorted and updated every day. Every task is captured into this list, so that the client can automatically proceed to the next task in order of priority.

2. Organize Projects into Tasks:

    Divide projects, those requiring multiple tasks, into separate tasks. For example, a project might be, "Write observation notes for the fourth-grade team," and a task might be, "Write the observation notes for the Tuesday observation of Ms. Smithers."

3. Daily Accountability:

    Reflect on daily task completion. You cannot have more than six "A" priorities. If you have more, then the same high-priority tasks will occur every day and you will feel that you are not making any progress.

APPENDIX F.
LEADING COLLABORATIVE TEAMS OF TEACHERS AND ADMINISTRATORS CHECKLIST

This form is not designed to provide an evaluative score; rather, it is to provide specific feedback for collaborative teams.

School district:
School name:
Date:
Coach:
Meeting type:
Grade level:
Subject:
Collaborative Team (CT) Expectation Criteria Ratings:

- A *1)* is an emerging CT that is beginning to show signs of being effective.
- A *2)* represents a progressing CT, one that is moving toward effective practices.
- A *3)* is an effective CT.
- A *4)* is given to a distinguished CT that is highly adaptive and showcases progressive practices.

Focus Area One—Meeting Norms, Agendas, and Roles of Team Members:

Meeting norms are established and revisited at each meeting and known by all members of the team.

1. Norms are not yet established.
2. Norms are established and referenced but not yet used for group behavior.
3. Norms are known by all team members, discussed at the start of each meeting, and followed throughout the meeting.

4. Norms are established, revisited, and adapted to determine effectiveness.

Meeting has an established agenda team members follow.

1. Agenda is not yet being used.
2. Agenda is available but not yet guiding the meeting.
3. Agenda is available to all members, used to guide the meeting, and includes actionable plans for the team.
4. Agenda preview is available beforehand to all members to obtain input, used to guide the meeting, and includes actionable plans for the team. Agendas are formatted consistently.

Each member of the team has a role (e.g., facilitator, recorder, reporter, time-keeper, etc.). Roles are fluid and are rotated regularly.

1. Roles are not yet established.
2. Roles are established but not yet used for meeting efficiency.
3. Each team member is held accountable for their individual role, working to continually focus on efficiency and effectiveness.
4. Roles are established, regularly rotated, and filled by volunteers from the group. Team members hold each other accountable for their role and the efficiency of the group.

Focus Area Two—Identification of Learning Intentions and Tier-1 Instruction:

Learning intentions are mutually agreed upon by team members, and all are able to answer the question: What is it we want students to know and be able to do, relevant to the identified learning intention/standard?

1. Learning intentions are not yet established by the team.
2. Learning intentions are established but not yet being used for instruction.

3. Team members agree on the learning intention/standard and create success criteria.
4. The language used in the success criteria successfully combines the language of the standards, rigor, and implementation.

Tier-1 instruction is identified by the team based upon the mutually agreed upon expectations for student performance within the identified learning intention/standard. Team members perform this by asking and answering the following question: "How will we teach and assess this learning intention/standard?"

1. Team cannot clearly define quality Tier-1 instruction.
2. Team does not clearly distinguish Tier-1, Tier-2, and Tier-3 instruction while identifying how to teach and/or assess the learning intention/standard.
3. Tier-1 instruction is consistently applied for instructional planning within the team, based upon the identified learning intention/standard.
4. Tier-1 instruction is consistently aligned to the correct level of rigor of the learning intention/standard for both instruction and assessment, which includes clear plans for differentiation.

Focus Area Three—Evidence of Student Understanding:
Team members arrive at the meeting with evidence of student understanding (data) relevant to the proposed learning intention/standard.

1. Team members are not yet coming to meetings prepared and do not have student evidence/data.
2. Team members arrive at meeting with student evidence/data, but the data is not of high quality or actionable.
3. High quality student evidence/data that provides insights into actionable entry points for intervention and enrichment is consistently brought to meetings by all team members.

4. Multiple sources of student evidence/data are reviewed during team meetings, which serves to triangulate or better solidify understandings of student performance and trends over time.

Evidence of student understanding is of inherent value to the team's discussion, which includes differentiated instruction.

1. Team discussion does not yet include plans for differentiation.
2. Team discussion includes reference to differentiated instruction but without actionable plans.
3. Team discussion includes evidence/data of learning that is consistently aligned with learning intentions/standards and includes plans for differentiation.
4. Team discussion is consistently efficient, with predetermined sources of evidence of student understanding/data (which include trends of student performance over time), allowing for in-depth discussions of differentiated learning needs to include preventative instruction.

Opportunities for collaborative scoring of student work among the team are present, which enables teacher calibration of expectations for student performance.

1. Team does not yet collaboratively score assessments.
2. Team collaboratively scores some samples of evidence/data but not yet with consistency and lacking alignment of expectations.
3. Team members bring samples of student work on an assigned task to the meeting. The team actively engages in collaborative scoring and evaluating the work, using a common rubric. The team works to reach consensus as a means of calibrating team member expectations.
4. All team members bring student work to the meeting and quickly engage in a collaborative scoring protocol. Team members examine a single piece of student work and individually

evaluate that work, using a common rubric. When there are differences, team members discuss them and work to reach consensus to calibrate expectations as well as a means to create data trends and adapt instruction.

Focus Area Four—Team Planning for Intervention and Enrichment Activities:

Team works together to design intervention activities using research-based strategies for students who do not demonstrate proficiency.

1. Team is not yet planning for intervention.
2. Team identifies need for intervention and chooses strategies to be implemented.
3. Team identifies intervention activities sourced from past successful practices and/or new learning from outside sources aligned with the learning deficit(s) identified.
4. Team has a repository of intervention strategies that is accessible to everyone grounded in research-based best practices, aligned with learning deficit(s) identified for the population of students served within the school.

Team works together to design enrichment opportunities for students who already demonstrate an understanding of the content.

1. Team is not yet planning enrichment activities and/or assigning additional work for students who already demonstrate proficiency.
2. Team plans for enrichment activities without scaffolding rigor for increased expectations.
3. Team identifies enrichment activities sourced from past successful practices and/or new learning from outside sources focused on the scaffolding of rigor.

4. Team has a repository of enrichment activities that focuses on higher degrees of rigor within the learning intention/standard while also promoting project-based activities.

The instructional delivery timelines of both intervention and enrichment activities are understood by team members with a plan to review student performance at a later date.

1. Team has not yet developed timelines for intervention or enrichment.
2. Team has identified a possible timeline for the delivery of instruction, without clear intervals, or planning for the review of student work.
3. Team members are clear on a timeline to implement instructional strategies and have a scheduled date to revisit evidence of student understanding.
4. Team members maintain timelines for the delivery of instructional strategies, allowing for possible adaptation based upon student performance while consistently reviewing student work as a team.

Focus Area Five—Team Reporting and Feedback:
At the conclusion of the meeting, all team members depart with meeting notes that include actionable plans for student learning.

1. Team has not yet developed actionable plans.
2. Team has developed actionable plans, but it is not noted in the minutes.
3. Based on team action plans, each member is clear on next steps (e.g., instruction, data review, etc.), which is reported in meeting notes.
4. Based on team action plans, each member consistently reflects upon action steps and adjusts as necessary between meetings while communicating with other team members and building leadership.

There is an established reporting process used to communicate team meeting notes/decisions that are shared with building leadership teams.

1. Team has not yet developed a process for communication.
2. Team has developed a process for communication but does not regularly use it.
3. Team continuously utilizes the identified reporting process, ensuring that the building leadership team receives timely updates.
4. Team continuously utilizes the identified reporting process, ensuring that the building leadership team receives timely updates and highlights needs for professional development.

Ongoing feedback between the PLC team and building leadership is evident as a means to continue to enhance professional practices as well as to understand student performance.

1. Reciprocal feedback is not yet developed in the organization.
2. Reciprocal feedback is provided inconsistently.
3. Reciprocal feedback follows an established timeline to gather data to make decisions and is reflected on during meetings.
4. Reciprocal feedback is continuously reviewed/reflected upon and referenced during staff meetings as a means of sharing leadership while encouraging data-based decisions for the building overall.

Comments:

APPENDIX G.
LEADING INDICATORS CHECKLIST

Relevance: The leading indicator is evidence-based and directly linked to one or more of our results goals. Chapter 14 provides a good place to start for examples of leading indicators.

Accountability: The leading indicator focuses on the specific and observable actions of teachers and leaders.

Control: The leading indicator is completely within our control; we can decide to take the actions that lead to the accomplishment of this indicator.

APPENDIX H.
CLASSROOM OBSERVATION CHECKLIST

This checklist's intent is to provide feedback to teachers regarding high quality. Consider focusing on how to expand criteria, including anchoring to expectations, looking for evidence of the criteria, provision of specific and actionable feedback, and planning for support.

- ☐ Clear and visible learning targets are evident in the classroom.
- ☐ Students understand the learning targets.
- ☐ Learning targets align with state standards.
- ☐ All students are on-task and can explain to the observer what the next action will be when they complete their present task.
- ☐ There are visible examples of proficient work.
- ☐ There is clear evidence of student thinking and understanding, rather than teacher-centered instruction.
- ☐ There is clear evidence of a learning goal for each student.
- ☐ There is evidence of formative feedback—that is, written and oral assessments and checks for understanding that lead to immediate improvements in teaching and learning.
- ☐ There is evidence of strong relationships among students and teachers; they know one another's names and offer positive reinforcement without prompting.
- ☐ There is evidence in small-group work that students understand their roles, learn from one another, provide feedback to one another, and provide a positive and mutually reinforcing environment.
- ☐ There is real-world application.
- ☐ Teacher moves around the room, especially close to students who are disengaged or potentially disruptive.
- ☐ Teacher and students provide immediate and specific feedback.
- ☐ Students make clear and specific reference to the texts and teaching from the lesson.
- ☐ There is evidence of student writing in every subject, and evidence of editing and rewriting.

ABOUT THE AUTHOR AND CONTRIBUTORS

Douglas Reeves is the author of more than 40 books and 100 articles on education and leadership. Twice named to the Harvard University Distinguished Authors Series, Doug was selected by *Consulting Magazine* as one of the top five leadership consultants in the United States for 2021. His career of service in education led to the Contribution to the Field Award from the National Staff Development Council, the Brock International Prize, and the William Walker Award from the Australian Council of Educational Leaders. He is the founder of Creative Leadership Solutions and has worked in 50 states and more than 40 countries.

* * *

Lisa Almeida is the Executive Director at Creative Leadership Solutions. She is a recognized educator with 20 years of experience delivering professional development and implementation support to educators. Most notably, Lisa is known for effective leadership and teacher coaching in the areas of standards, assessment, systems development, and professional learning communities. She is a contributing author to several publications and is honored to be a part of such a timely resource. Lisa is a consummate advocate for quality public education for all, including for her children—Sofia, Moises IV, and Max.

Tony Flach brings a lifetime of experience to his work leading change to improve outcomes for students in schools and districts across the country. He grew up in his mother's classroom and went on to become a teacher, instructional coach, and administrator in Norfolk, Virginia, public schools and to marry another educator. Tony believes that a quality education is the cornerstone for social equity and is passionate about supporting practices to improve student achievement. The use of data at all levels drives successful implementation. Tony has worked with clients to launch initiatives and create systems to monitor and refine those actions in real time. His experience includes leadership roles in a Broad Prize award-winning district, work at two educational publishers, and more than 20 years of coaching and consulting. He has experienced firsthand the difference that effective teachers, schools, and systems make in a community and believes that every school can and should be a place that he would want his own children to attend.

Kate Anderson Foley is a lifetime learner and advocate for those whose voices are not always heard. She is kind but powerful, with a laser focus on accomplishing big goals.

Kate is a transformational leader with deep experience at all levels of the education organization. She has partnered with local, state, and national organizations; education agencies; and industries—providing her expertise with the improvement process, strategic planning, equity-based funding, policies, and practices. Kate has worked closely with senior leadership across various sectors providing executive coaching aimed at creating strength-based organizational cultures. She has presented nationally and internationally and has authored many publications.

Amanda Gomez is a dedicated educator with more than 20 years of experience, including classroom teaching, instructional coaching, professional development, and instructional design. She is passionate about providing professional development and coaching that improves classroom instruction and student engagement leading to high levels of student achievement, especially in mathematics. She believes all students can reach success through effective instruction. Amanda currently provides effective leadership and teacher coaching in the areas of leadership, professional learning communities, effective instruction, standards, and assessment.

The Creative Leadership Solutions Coaching Tool Kit was created and developed by Jo Peters. Jo is a highly recognized Leadership Performance Coach. She provides executive and leadership coaching to building- and district-level leaders, helping them reach high levels of performance and create sustainable change within their organizations. Jo has supported leaders nationwide and volunteered her coaching expertise to educators in Zambia and high-poverty schools. A former teacher, instructional coach, principal, and principal supervisor—she is a skilled presenter and facilitator and a contributing author to several publications on formative assessment, school improvement, and coaching techniques and strategies.

Bill Sternberg has more than 20 years of experience in education as a former special education teacher, elementary principal, state-level director and assistant superintendent. He currently works nationally with teacher and administrative teams in various coaching capacities focused on the enhancement of professional practice. Bill attributes much of his success to the inspiration to make learning more engaging provided by his three children—Tyler, Noah, and Addison.

REFERENCES

Amabile, T. M., & Kramer, S. J. (2011). "The power of small wins." *Harvard Business Review, 89*(5), 70–81.

Agarwal, P., & Bain, P. M. (2019). *Powerful Teaching: Unleash The Science of Learning.* Wiley.

Axtell, P. (2018, June 22). "The most productive meetings have fewer than 8 people." *Harvard Business Review.* https://hbr.org/2018/06/the-most-productive-meetings-have-fewer-than-8-people

Bae, K.-Y., Kang, H.-J., Kim, J.-M., Kim, S.-W., Shin, H.-Y., Shin, I.-S., & J.-S., Yoon, (2014). "Impact of anxiety and depression on physical health condition and disability in an elderly Korean population." *Psychiatry Investigation, 14*(3), 240–248. https://doi.org/10.4306/pi.2017.14.3.240

Bauer, M., Damschroder, L., Hagedorn, H., Smith, J., & Kilbourne, A. (2015). "An introduction to implementation science for the non-specialist." *BMC Psychology, 3*(1). https://doi.org/doi:10.1186/s40359-015-0089-9

Boser, U. (2022, February 3). "Retrieval practice: The five things you need to know about retrieval practice." The Learning Agency Lab. https://www.the-learning-agency-lab.com/learning-strategies/retrieval-practice/

Boynton, A. (2016, March 31). "Nine things that separate the leaders from the managers." Forbes. https://www.forbes.com/sites/andyboynton/2016/03/31/want-to-be-a-leader-not-just-a-manager-do-these-nine-things/?sh=506a23ec51e0

Brantlinger, A. (2021). "Entering, staying, shifting, leaving, and sometimes returning: A descriptive analysis of the career trajectories of two cohorts of alternatively certified mathematics teachers." *Sage Journals/Teachers College Record*, *123*(9), 28–56. https://journals.sagepub.com/doi/10.1177/01614681211051996

Buckingham, M., & Goodall, A. (2019). *Nine Lies About Work: A Freethinking Leader's Guide to the Real World*. Harvard Business Review Press.

Burns, R. "To a louse, on seeing one on a lady's bonnet at church" (1786), in *Poems and Songs of Robert Burns*. (2018, March 15). [eBook]. Project Gutenberg Literary Archive Foundation. Retrieved May 16, 2021, from https://www.gutenberg.org/files/1279/1279-h/1279-h.htm#2H_4_0107

Caron, C. (2021, February 17). "Nobody has openings: Mental health providers struggle to meet demand." *The New York Times*, 7.

Centers for Disease Control and Prevention. (2020, June 29). "Adult obesity facts: Obesity is a common, serious, and costly disease." https://www.cdc.gov/obesity/data/adult.html

Chen, Irene. (2020). "The importance of school leadership to teacher and student success." Overdeck Family Foundation.Org. https://overdeck.org/news-and-resources/article/the-importance-of-school-leadership-to-teacher-and-student-success/

Chenoweth, K. (2017). *Schools That Succeed: How Educators Marshal the Power of Systems for Improvement*. Harvard Education Press.

Clancy, C. (2020). "Treating depression with cognitive behavioral therapy." JourneyPure https://journeypureriver.com/treating-depression-cognitive-behavioral-therapy/

Clear, J. (2018). *Atomic Habits: An Easy & Proven Way to Build Good Habits & Break Bad Ones*. Avery/Penguin Random House.

Collado, W. (2021). *Beyond Conversations About Race: A Guide for Discussions with Students, Teachers, and Communities (How to*

Talk About Racism in Schools and Implement Equitable Classroom Practices). Solution Tree Press.

Conversano, C., Rotondo, A., Lensi, E., Della Vista, O., Arpone, F., & Reda, M. A. (2010). "Optimism and its impact on mental and physical well-being." *Clinical Practice & Epidemiology in Mental Health*, 2010(6), 25–29. https://doi.org/10.2174/1745017901006010025

Cook, A., & Moore, M. (2020, February 22). "What to do if your client seems stressed." Institute of Coaching. https://instituteofcoaching.org/resources/what-do-if-your-client-seems-stressed

Covey, Stephen. (2020). *The 7 Habits of Highly Effective People* (30th anniversary ed.). Simon & Schuster.

DiAngelo, R., & Dyson, M. E. (2018). *White Fragility: Why It's So Hard for White People to Talk About Racism*. Beacon Press.

Doerr, J. (2018). *Measure What Matters: How Google, Bono, and The Gates Foundation Rock The World With OKRS*. Portfolio Penguin.

Donahoo, J., Hattie, J., & Fells, R. (2018). "The power of collective efficacy." *Educational Leadership*, 75(6), 40–44.

Duening, T. N. (2018, October 8). "Nothing worth knowing can be taught." Wordpress. https://philosophyofflourishing.wordpress.com/2018/10/08/nothing-worth-learning-can-be-taught/

DuFour, R., DuFour, R., Eaker, R., & Many, T. W. (2006). *Learning By Doing: A Handbook for Professional Learning Communities at Work*. Solution Tree Press.

DuFour, R., & Reeves, D. (2016). "The futility of PLC Lite." *Phi Delta Kappan*, 97(6), 69–71.

DuFour, R., DuFour, R., & Reeves, D. (2017). *Responding to the Every Student Succeeds Act with the PLC at Work ™ process*. Solution Tree Press.

Eckfeldt, B. (2019, June 27). "There are many types of coaches. Here's how to find the right one." Inc. https://www.inc.com/bruce-eckfeldt/there-are-many-types-of-coaches-heres-how-to-find-right-one.html

Edmondson, A. C. (2018). *The Fearless Organization: Creating Psychological Safety in the Workplace for Learning, Innovation, and Growth.* Wiley.

Eva, A. L. (2017, November 28). "Why we should embrace mistakes in school." *Greater Good Magazine.* https://greatergood.berkeley.edu/article/item/why_we_should_embrace_mistakes_in_school

Family Education Staff. (2019, May 15). "When teens obsess about their weight." *familyeducation.* https://www.familyeducation.com/life/body-image/when-teens-obsess-about-their-weight

Fogg, B. J. (2021). *Tiny Habits: The Small Changes That Change Everything.* HarperCollins.

Frankl, V. (1946). *Man's Search For Meaning.* Beacon Press.

Goldstein, D. (2022, March 8). "It's 'alarming': children are severely behind in reading." *The New York Times.* https://www.nytimes.com/2022/03/08/us/pandemic-schools-reading-crisis.html?referringSource=articleShare

Goleman, Daniel. (2013). *Focus: The Hidden Driver Of Excellence.* HarperCollins.

Grant, A. M., & Atad, O. I. (2021). "Coaching psychology interventions vs. positive psychology interventions: The measurable benefits of a coaching relationship." *The Journal of Positive Psychology, 17*(4), 532–534. https://doi.org/10.1080/17439760.2021.1871944

Gregersen, H. (2018, March–April). "Better brainstorming: Focus on questions, not answers, for breakthrough insights." *Harvard Business Review,* 64–71. https://hbr.org/2018/03/better-brainstorming

Grissom, J. A., Egalite, A. J., & Lindsay, C. (2021). "How principals affect students and schools: A systematic synthesis of two decades of research." The Wallace Foundation. https://www.wallacefoundation.org/knowledge-center/Documents/How-Principals-Affect-Students-and-Schools.pdf

Gupta, S. (2022, January 24). "What is school violence?" Verywell Mind. https://www.verywellmind.com/school-violence-types-causes-impact-and-prevention-5216631

Guskey, T. (2021). "The past and future of teacher efficacy." *Educational Leadership, 79*(3), 20–25.

Hamilton, A., Reeves, D., Clinton, J., & Hattie, J. (2022). *Building To Impact: The 5D Implementation Playbook for Educators*. Corwin Press.

Hari, J. (2022). *Stolen Focus: Why You Can't Pay Attention—and How to Think Deeply Again*. Crown Business.

Hattie, J. (2013). *Visible Learning For Teachers: Maximizing Impact on Learning*. Taylor & Francis.

Hattie, J., & Yates, G. (2014). *Visible Learning and the Science of How We Learn*. Routledge.

Hess, F. (2018, June 12). "Education Reformers Should Obey Campbell's Law." Education Next. https://www.education-next.org/education-reforms-obey-campbells-law/

Imberman, S. (2015, June). "How effective are financial incentives for teachers?" IZA World of Labor. https://wol.iza.org/uploads/articles/158/pdfs/how-effective-are-financial-incentives-for-teachers.pdf

Kahneman, D. (2013). *Thinking, Fast and Slow*. Farrar, Straus and Giroux.

Klapisch, B. (2019, September 6). "The dying art of the manager meltdown." *The New York Times*, 11.

Konnikova, M. (2020). *The Biggest Bluff: How I Learned to Pay Attention, Master Myself, and Win.* Penguin Press.

Kouzes, J. M., & Posner, B. Z. (2011). *Credibility: How Leaders Gain and Lose It; Why People Demand It.* Jossey-Bass.

Kuhfeld, M., & Tarasawa, B. (2020, April). The COVID-19 slide: "What summer learning loss can tell us about the potential impact of school closures on student academic achievement." NWEA. https://www.nwea.org/content/uploads/2020/05/Collaborative-Brief_Covid19-Slide-APR20.pdf

Lafley, A. G., & Martin, R. L. (2013). *Playing To Win: How Strategy Really Works.* Harvard Business Review Press.

Ledford, G. E., Gearhart, B., & Fang, M. (2013, 2nd quarter). "Negative Effects of Extrinsic Rewards on Intrinsic Motivation: More Smoke Than Fire." *WorldatWork Journal.* http://www.formapex.com/telechargementpublic/ledford2013a.pdf

Leslie, I. (2021). *Conflicted: How Productive Disagreements Lead to Better Outcomes.* Harper-Collins.

MacKie, D. (2016). *Strength-Based Leadership Coaching in Organizations: An Evidence-Based Guide to Positive Leadership Development.* Kogan-Page.

Mankins, M., & Garton, E. (2017). *Time, Talent, Energy: Overcome Organizational Drag and Unleash Your Team's Productive Power.* Harvard Business Review Press.

Marshall, K. (2013). *Rethinking Teacher Supervision and Education: How to Work Smart, Build Collaboration, and Close the Achievement Gap* (2nd ed.). Jossey-Bass.

Marshall, K. (2019, February 20). "Rethinking the way we coach, evaluate, and appreciate teachers." Fordham Institute. https://fordhaminstitute.org/national/commentary/rethinking-way-we-coach-evaluate-and-appreciate-teachers

Marzano, R. J. (2017). *The New Art and Science of Teaching.* ASCD/Solution Tree.

Mitropoulos, A. (2021, June 11*).* "With return to in-person learning, thousands of students still 'missing' from schools." [Video]. ABC News. https://abcnews.go.com/Health/return-person-learning-thousands-students-missing-schools/story?id=78051068

Moore, M. (2020, October 25). "Peak coaching moments." Institute of Coaching. https://instituteofcoaching.org/resources/peak-coaching-moments

Neason, A. (2017). "Does homework help?" *ASCD Education Update, 50*(1). http://www.ascd.org/publications/newsletters/education-update/jan17/vol59/num01/Does-Homework-Help¢.aspx

Newport, C. (2016). *Deep Work: Rules for Focused Success in a Distracted World.* Grand Central Publishing.

Newport, C. (2021). *A World Without Email: Reimagining Work in an Age of Communication Overload.* Portfolio/Penguin.

Osborn, A. F. (1953). *Applied Imagination: Principles and Procedures of Creative Thinking.* Charles Scribner's Sons.

Pascal, B. (1658). "Les provinciales [The mystery of jesuitisme…]." (J. Evelyn? Trans.; 2nd ed. corrected). Letter 16, 292. R. Royston.

Peters, J., & Carr, C. (2015, January 7). "Team effectiveness and team coaching literature review." Institute of Coaching. https://instituteofcoaching.org/resources/team-effectiveness-and-team-coaching-literature-review

Peterson, D., & Johnson, W. (2017, January 5). "Executive coaching on the cusp of disruption: what's up with the mashup?" Institute of Coaching. https://instituteofcoaching.org/resources/executive-coaching-cusp-disruption-whats-mashup

Reeves, D. (2008). *Assessing Educational Leaders: Evaluating Performance for Improved Individual and Organizational Results* (2nd ed.). Corwin Press.

Reeves, D. (2009). *Leading Change in Your School: How to Conquer Myths, Build Commitment, and Get Results.* ASCD.

Reeves, D. (2013). *Finding Your Leadership Focus: What Matters Most for Student Results.* Columbia University Teachers College Press.

Reeves, D. (2016). *From Leading to Succeeding: The Seven Elements of Effective Leadership in Education.* Solution Tree Press.

Reeves, D. (2018). "Seven keys to restoring the teacher pipeline." *Educational Leadership, 75*(8). http://www.ascd.org/publications/educational-leadership/may18/vol75/num08/Seven-Keys-to-Restoring-the-Teacher-Pipeline.aspx

Reeves, D. (2019). "Dramatic turnaround in one semester: Another case of 100-day leaders." *Creative Leadership Solutions.* https://www.creativeleadership.net/blog/2019/2/16/dramatic-turnaround-in-one-semester-another-case-of-100-day-leaders?rq=failures

Reeves, D. (2020a). *Achieving Equity and Excellence: Immediate Results from the Lessons of High-Poverty, High-Success Schools.* Solution Tree Press.

Reeves, D. (2020b). *The Learning Leader: How to Focus School Improvement for Better Results.* Association for Supervision & Curriculum Development.

Reeves, D. (2020c). "Supercharged cabinet meetings: Establishing norms, recording commitments and requiring evidence for the body of senior leaders who advise the superintendent." AASA School Administrator.

Reeves, D. (2021). *Deep Change Leadership: A Model for Renewing and Strengthening Schools and Districts.* Solution Tree Press.

Reeves, D. (2023). *Fearless Schools* (rev. ed.). Creative Leadership Press/Archway Publishing.

Reeves, D. B. (2016). *Elements of Grading: A Guide to Effective Practice* (2nd ed.). Solution Tree Press.

Reeves, D. B. (2021). *The Learning Leader: How to Focus School Improvement for Better Results* (2nd ed.). Association for Supervision & Curriculum Development.

Reeves, D., & Eaker, R. (2019). *100-Day Leaders: Turning Short-Term Wins into Long-Term Success in Schools*. Solution Tree Press.

Reuell, P. (2019, September 4). "Lessons in learning." *Harvard Gazette*. https://news.harvard.edu/gazette/story/2019/09/study-shows-that-students-learn-more-when-taking-part-in-classrooms-that-employ-active-learning-strategies/

Roberts, W. (1990). *Leadership Secrets of Attila the Hun*. Grand Central Publishing.

Rodin, J. (2014). *The Resilience Dividend: Being Strong in a World Where Things Go Wrong*. PublicAffairs.

Rogelberg, S. G. (2019). *The Surprising Science of Meetings: How You Can Lead Your Team to Peak Performance*. Oxford University Press.

Salzberg, S. (2020). *Real Change: Mindfulness to Heal Ourselves and the World*. Flatiron Books.

Schorr, A., Carter, C., & Ladiges, W. (2018). "The potential use of physical resilience to predict healthy aging." *Pathobiology of Aging & Age-Related Diseases, 8*(1). https://doi.org/10.1080/20010001.2017.1403844

Seligman, M. E. P. (2006). *Learned Optimism: How to Change Your Mind and Your Life*. Knopf Doubleday.

Seligman, M. E. P. (2007). *The Optimistic Child: A Proven Program to Safeguard Children Against Depression and Build Lifelong Resilience*. Mariner Books.

Sherman, S., & Freas, A. (2004, November). "The wild west of executive coaching." *Harvard Business Review*. https://hbr.org/2004/11/the-wild-west-of-executive-coaching

"Sleep and mental health: Sleep deprivation can affect your mental health." (2021, August 17). *Harvard Health Publishing/Harvard Medical School*. https://www.health.harvard.edu/newsletter_article/sleep-and-mental-health

Snow, S. (2020, April 23). "The Counterintuitive Thing About Trust That Explains Why So Many Teams Have Issues With It." *Linked-in*. https://www.linkedin.com/pulse/counterintuitive-thing-trust-explains-why-so-many-teams-shane-snow/?trk=eml-email_series_follow_newsletter_01-hero-1-title_link&midToken=AQFCemYK6DrsgA&fromEmail=fromEmail&ut=1mT3a61j4Npc1&utm_source=ActiveCampaign&utm_medi

Sparks, S. D. (2016, November 1). "Principals Work 60-Hour Weeks, Study Finds." Education Week. https://www.edweek.org/leadership/principals-work-60-hour-weeks-study-finds/2016/11

Stenger, M. (2014, August 6). "5 Researched-Based Tips for Providing Students Meaningful Feedback." George Lucas Educational Foundation Edutopia. https://www.edutopia.org/blog/tips-providing-students-meaningful-feedback-marianne-stenger

Syed, M. (2021). *Rebel Ideas: The Power of Diverse Thinking*. Flatiron Books.

U.S. Department of Education. (2022, March 28). "U.S. Education Secretary Miguel Cardona Calls on States, Districts, Higher Ed Institutions to Address Nationwide Teacher Shortage and Bolster Student Recovery with American Rescue Plan Funds." [Press Release]. https://www.ed.gov/news/press-releases/us-education-secretary-miguel-cardona-calls-states-districts-higher-ed-institutions-address-nationwide-teacher-shortage-and-bolster-student-recovery-american-rescue-plan-funds

Wilding, M. (2021, May 31). "Stop Being So Hard on Yourself." *Harvard Business Review*. https://hbr.org/2021/05/stop-being-so-hard-on-yourself?utm_medium=email&utm_source=newsletter_daily&utm_campaign=dailyalert_notactsubs&deliveryName=DM134831

Willingham, D. T. (2021). *Why Don't Students Like School: A Cognitive Scientist Answers Questions About How the Mind Works and What It Means for the Classroom* (2nd ed.). Wiley.

Wiseman, L. (2010). *Multipliers: How the Best Leaders Make Everyone Smarter*. HarperBusiness.

Yang, C., Boen, C., Gerken, K., Ting, L., & Schorpp, K. (2016). "Social relationships and physiological determinants of longevity across the human life span." *Proceedings of the National Academy of Sciences, 113*(3), 578–583. https://doi.org/10.1073/pnas.1511085112

Zaleznik, A. (1992, April). "Leaders And Managers: Are They Different?" *Harvard Business Review*. https://hbr.org/1992/03/managers-and-leaders-are-they-different-2

Printed in the USA
CPSIA information can be obtained
at www.ICGtesting.com
LVHW100734170823
755368LV00001B/1